Brasseur & Eisler

BRASSEUR

& EISLER

To Catch a Dream

As told to
Lynda D. Prouse

Macmillan Canada
Toronto

Canadian Cataloguing in Publication Data

Prouse, Lynda, D.
Brasseur & Eisler : to catch a dream

Includes index.
ISBN 0-7715-7393-6

1. Brasseur, Isabelle. 2. Eisler, Lloyd. 3. Skating – Canada.
4. Skaters – Canada – Biography. I. Title.

GV850.A2P76 1996   796.91'2'092271   c96–930958–9

Macmillan Canada wishes to thank the Canada Council, the
Ontario Arts Council and the Ontario Ministry of Culture and
Communications for supporting its publishing program.

Jacket and text design: Gord Robertson
Cover photo: F. Scott Grant/Canadian Sports Images

Macmillan Canada
A Division of Canada Publishing Corporation
Toronto, Canada

1 2 3 4 5   00 99 98 97 96

Printed in Canada

To Lloyd, who is the other half of this book. Without you, I would never have made it this far. Thank you for your support during the difficult and sad times and also for sharing so much happiness with me. The memories will be in my heart for the rest of my life and I hope we will continue to share in the coming years. Always remember that your little "Freddy" will be there for you.

ISABELLE BRASSEUR

This book is dedicated to my strength, my partner and my best friend, Isabelle "Fred" Brasseur, who gave me the opportunity to realize a dream and who stood by my side when others were nowhere to be found. Thank you for the memories, the emotions and your friendship.

LLOYD EISLER

To my family, especially my sister Marlene and my dear parents, Bob and Vera Prouse, for their constant love and guidance, and to my husband and best friend, David Szabo, who always believed in my dreams. A sincere thank you to Lloyd and Isabelle for taking me on their journey.

LYNDA D. PROUSE

ACKNOWLEDGEMENTS

Thank you, Lynda, for helping us make this book a reality. You made it pretty easy on us; Josée and Eric, who have always guided me in the right direction and who I am happy to call my good friends; Dad, Mom, Dom and Josée, for your love and support; all my friends—just for being my friends. Last, but not least, I would like to thank our fans for supporting and cheering us on!

ISABELLE BRASSEUR

I want to thank my parents, Beverley and Lloyd, who are the most wonderful mother and father a son could have; my sisters Marie and Mary Jane, who sacrificed a lot to see me reach my dreams; my first coach, Kerry Leitch, who believed in my talent and gave me the right direction to achieve my goals; my present coaches, Josée Picard and Eric Gillies, who guided the bull through the china shop without breaking too many things and who always believed Isabelle and I had what it takes to reach the top of the mountain; my long-time friends, Pam and John Boniferro, who were always there to remind me of the real world and where I had come from—their shoulders were always there for me to cry on when things seemed at their worst; Dr. Peter Jensen, who was there when we needed guidance through the tough times; our choreographers, Uschi Keszler and Julie Marcotte, who gave us the creativity to put together great programs for competitions and exhibitions; my first partner, Lorri Baier, who taught me the skills of leadership and gave me the confidence to always move forward; the Canadian Figure Skating Association for their long-time support; our agents, Yuki Saegusa and Jay Ogden, for believing in us enough to take a chance on our careers; Lynda Prouse for giving us the opportunity to tell our story; Dr. Wendy Jerome, who from the very beginning believed in me and my quest to make a difference; Lou-Ann Brosseau, our partner in BBE Productions; my friend Pam Carnochan, who gave me the spiritual strength to continue the journey; and to all those who in some way have touched my life and taught me lessons that will never be forgotten—thank you.

LLOYD EISLER

Many thanks to the staff of Macmillan Canada for their efforts to put out the best book possible, especially editor Nicole de Montbrun and publisher, Karen O'Reilly.

LYNDA D. PROUSE

CONTENTS

17th Olympic Winter Games, Lillehammer

Lloyd & Isabelle

THE AIRPLANE was nearing its destination of Oslo and the competition that would be the climax of our amateur skating career. We were entering the event as the reigning world champions and were pitted against two Russian teams, both Olympic gold medalists.

When we first heard the ruling that professional skaters would be contending at the Olympics, we were upset because throughout Olympic history only amateurs had been allowed to compete. It was finally our turn to have the opportunity to become Olympic champions and we had to skate against the pros. Since the pros had won gold before, they would have to perform very poorly to fall down in the standings—the skating world is just too political for an upset.

Yet, there were some good points to the ruling as well—it made us work that much harder. We also believed that this would be the most exciting pairs competition in the past decade and for years to come.

Thanks to a huge turnaround in our attitudes toward skating, and life in general, the outcome didn't seem to matter—a far cry from the feelings we had had in Albertville only two years before. This time we were going to enjoy ourselves and perform for the fans who had been so loyal to us over the years. When the Olympics were over, we wanted to know that we had done the best we could possibly do and to leave our amateur career feeling good about ourselves.

Lloyd

Norway's snowy landscape loomed below. I glanced over at Isabelle and smiled. There was and is a unique bond between us. It's a friendship that has stood the test of time and I wondered now how she was feeling. Was her rib bothering her? She had injured it at practice a couple of days before we left but had refused to get X rays. I opened my mouth to mention it but decided to keep my thoughts to myself. There was no point in bringing up anything negative when we were feeling so positive.

We began our descent into Oslo and I was getting more excited by the minute. For an athlete there is nothing like the Olympic Games to bring out so many emotions. It's difficult to explain how much pride you feel in being given the opportunity to represent your country at the Games, and we were definitely going to savor every moment of what would be our last Olympic experience.

Isabelle

As I tried to relax on the plane, I thought of the many memories that Lloyd and I shared.

I looked over at him and returned his smile but couldn't help noticing the concern in his eyes. He was probably worrying about my rib, which I hurt in practice just before we left. It wasn't the first time I had fractured a rib while doing the triple lateral. I had cracked it before so I knew what to expect. I declined to have X rays because I didn't want to know the damage. Competing at these Olympics was far too important to me and I was determined to be on the ice.

I hoped now that Lloyd wasn't giving the injury too much thought. My partner and best friend of nine years has always taken care of me, but since my dad passed away, Lloyd seemed to take on the role far more seriously. It's a good feeling knowing that we can rely on each other.

As the plane landed, I thought about what being an Olympian meant, how special it was and how I had vowed to enjoy these Games. Although there had been many ups and downs in my career, I had accomplished pretty much what I had wanted to. Now, one of my last goals was to win an Olympic medal and be proud of it, no matter the color.

Lloyd

On the night of the short-program competition, everyone else seemed to be more nervous than we were. Isabelle's dad was responsible for this inner calmness.

We had such a hard time after he died that we questioned whether it was worth continuing to skate. Getting through that experience taught us how to relax. Although I've never been the nervous type, I would still get edgy before a competition and Isabelle would get anxious, but after Gill's death our attitudes changed. We knew that our lives didn't depend on one four-minute program. We also realized that the people who loved us before we skated were still going to love us after we finished, whether we skated well, whether we won or whether we came last.

I smiled as I sat in the dressing room, knowing what Isabelle was doing at that very moment. She still holds on to one nervous habit before we go on the ice and that is to tie and retie her skates, over and over again.

She had assured me and our coaches that, despite her injury, she was ready to skate, and if Isabelle says she is ready, we absolutely trust her. I knew she would give it all she had because she is that type of person.

Isabelle

When Dad was alive, we were really close and he was very involved in my skating. I remember in Albertville, after I fell during our performance, he said he wished he could have been out there helping me. As I prepared for the competition, I "talked" to him the way I used to. I said, "Dad, come here a minute. All those years during my skating career, you said you wanted to help me and be out there skating for me, and now it's time." I knew he would be with me tonight just as I had sensed he was with me in Prague, when we won the world championship. This belief helped to settle my nerves.

When I arrived at the rink, I was glad that my coaches, Eric and Josée, were there. They make me laugh, especially Eric, who tells me all the jokes in the world.

We had decided not to tape my rib for the competition because the binding had really bothered me in practice. Everyone had been concerned as to whether or not I would be able to compete but I had told them that I was ready. I was prepared to skate through the pain just to be on the ice for our last Olympics.

Our names were about to be called for the warm-up so I watched for Lloyd; he has a tendency to wait until the last minute before coming out of the dressing room.

Lloyd

As they announced our names, I thought about this long and wonderful career I've had and the good and bad experiences I have shared with my partner. It had been a winding road with many interesting diversions and challenges along the way.

Right before we began our warm-up, I looked for my parents in the audience. I made eye contact with my father and he tipped his Stetson as if to say, "I'm here if you need me."

When it was time to begin the program, I took my best friend's hand and we skated to center ice. It was actually a relief to finally be out there. We had come so far, and as I listened to the thunderous applause and waited for the opening strains of our music, I knew beyond a doubt that if I had to live it all over again, there would be very little I would change.

Isabelle

As I took Lloyd's hand, I felt a surge of confidence. Both he and my dad were with me and we were ready. If only, I thought, we could achieve this last goal, it would make all the hard work, sacrifices and pain worth it.

I had been skating since I was six years old and somehow, despite the highs and lows, I had managed to reach this point in my career. Now here I was, standing at center ice, poised and ready to begin as millions of people around the world watched. Who would have thought, when I received that first pair of skates so many years ago, that it would result in this?

CHAPTER ONE

The Early Years

Isabelle

A CTUALLY, I hated that first pair of skates with a passion. Although I didn't begin figure skating until I was six, my mother had been taking my brother, Dominique, and I to the city to skate from the time I was about two.

The outings themselves are not very clear in my memory but I do remember those skates vividly. They were my brother's hand-me-downs and, because they were boys', they were brown. I was so embarrassed that I didn't have a white pair like the other little girls that I would refuse to take off my hat, which covered my hair. If I had to wear brown skates, then let them think I was a boy!

I was born in Kingsbury, Quebec, on July 28, 1970, the second and last child to Claudette and Gill. My parents and their parents are from the Montreal area, my mom being from Upton and my dad from St-Valerien. My grandpa on my dad's side was a proud man and hard worker who always strived for more. Not only did he invent a device to extract milk from cows but he also owned the first car in town.

Kingsbury was little more than a village, consisting of only a couple of streets and about twenty houses. Because of its size, everybody knew each other. It was so small that on Halloween all of the kids would meet at one place and trick-or-treat the whole town together.

Most of the residents, my dad included, were employed by the town's only large company, which made snowmobiles. We must have owned a snowmobile ourselves because I can recall Dad hooking up a buggy to the back of one and pulling Dominique and I around. When we lived in Kingsbury, Mom baby-sat other people's children during the day and both my parents were also employed at night at the restaurant of the local motel. They worked long hours but I never felt deprived of their time or their love.

My father and brother liked to play hockey and Mom skated for the sheer fun of it. Each year, Dad would flood the backyard of our house and that rink would be the town's ice. Everybody, including kids of all ages, would come and skate at our place, whether for a game of hockey or just for pleasure.

I cherish those early memories of my childhood in rural Quebec. Little did I know then how the physical closeness shared by my family would eventually take its toll on my emotions in its very absence. A simple decision that was soon to be made by my parents was about to change our lives.

Lloyd

My first recollection of skating is that I was terrible. I was six years old and couldn't skate if my life depended on it. I was all ankles and just awful. I'll never forget trying out for a hockey team and being told by the coach that they wouldn't allow me to play because I couldn't skate. To make matters worse, the first skates I owned were actually a girl's pair. They were white and my parents painted them black.

It wasn't planned that I was to be born in Seaforth, Ontario. My parents, Beverley-Ann and Lloyd Sr., and my older sister, Marie, were living in Nanaimo, British Columbia, where Dad was in the business of moving mobile homes. My father owned about five or six trucks and used to haul these trailers around the west coast. He and my mother, who was pregnant with me, decided to visit Seaforth because our relatives lived there. During their stay, Mom developed some problems and spent two and a half months in the hospital, bedridden. She had gained seventy-five pounds during her pregnancy, and when I was finally born on April 28, 1963, it must have been quite a relief to her. As soon as we were released from the hospital, my family returned to Nanaimo, where I lived happily until I was six years old.

I say happily because, to a child, what's not to like about living in the wilderness? Our home was a large trailer out in the bush and it was not unusual to wake up in the morning and see a mountain lion or bear in the front yard. There was no one else around, except for Kenny. He was my best friend and lived in the next trailer down the road. Kenny and I were inseparable. He is one of the few people I lost touch with and I sometimes wonder what became of my constant companion.

When I wasn't with Kenny, I would be traveling all over the countryside with my dad in one of his trucks. It was a great life for a kid but my parents, who are originally from Ontario, decided to pack up their family, which now included my younger sister, Mary Jane, and move us closer to our roots.

My father's parents were from Seaforth, where my dad was also born. I never met my father's dad as he died before I came into the world, but from what I understand the Eisler family was one of the first to settle in that area. Mom and her family were from Mitchell, about twelve miles down the road from Seaforth.

When we first arrived in Ontario, we stayed in Goderich with my dad's mother, who had just moved there. It was my kindergarten year and even way back then I was showing signs of being a pretty independent and inventive kid. I can remember being called into the principal's office because I had missed almost the entire afternoon of school. As usual, I'd been dillydallying on the way to class, stopping here and there for whatever attracted my interest at the moment and losing complete track of time in the process. When I finally arrived at school, I was sent straight to the office of the principal, who called my mother. I explained my tardiness by saying that after lunch Mom had made me clean up and do the dishes. I guess the principal got quite a kick out of the fact that, for one so young, I had come up with such a story. Shades of things to come, I suppose.

Seaforth, my parents' final destination, was a very small town with a population that has since grown to 2,000. When we arrived, the family settled into an apartment over top of a restaurant that my dad had purchased, and which was situated in the middle of town. It had five apartments upstairs and later Dad built a pool hall on the other side of the ground floor. I guess you could say that my parents were entrepreneurs. Both he and Mom ran the restaurant and eventually purchased another. These restaurants were the two biggest in town and I spent a lot of time there. In fact, that is where I learned to cook.

We lived in the apartment for a while and then moved to a large, old house. It had wooden floors and staircases that creaked and the place made spooky noises at night. For a kid with a big imagination, it was perfect.

We had only been in Seaforth a few months when I felt the sudden urge to play hockey. My mother's father, who we called Puppy, loved the sport and every Saturday night he would come to my house and take me back to his place to watch the game. My grandfather was my best friend in those days and I don't remember any part of my young life when he wasn't there for me.

No one else in our family was particularly athletic, except for Dad. As a youngster and a young man in the navy, he played all kinds of sports, including English rugger, baseball and hockey. Mom, on the other hand, was the more artistic of the two. She had taken ballet lessons throughout her early life, and skated a bit for pleasure.

Neither of them saw any reason why I should not play hockey and so, totally unaware of how this desire was about to alter my life, they bought me some skates and a stick and off to the rink we went.

Isabelle

When I was six years old, we moved to St-Jean-sur-Richelieu, where my mom still lives today. The town was much bigger than Kingsbury and it is where Dad had decided to open his own retreading company. While the plans for the company continued to develop, my parents were also having a house built and so we lived in an apartment for about a year.

St-Jean was great but I missed the ballet lessons that I had been taking in Kingsbury. Continuing them would have meant my parents driving twenty minutes to take me to class and they didn't want that. So they decided on figure skating instead because the rink was only five minutes from our home.

I adored the sport right away. The sensation of gliding and flowing on the ice was unlike any other feeling. You only had to give a little push and you would go so fast, without having to work too hard at it. I liked that.

Lloyd

I had so looked forward to playing hockey that when the coach said, "You can't play because you can't skate," I was devastated. He told me that before I could join the team I had to learn how to skate. In those days, there was no such thing as power skating. Either you played hockey or you figure skated.

Aside from the fact that I was from British Columbia and hadn't seen ice before, I also had a problem with my feet. I wore orthopedic shoes that were actually more like boots. They were the ugliest things and I had to wear them until I was about nine. I hated those shoes. I never owned a pair of runners or dress shoes, only those ugly boots that I had to wear.

When the coach told me I couldn't play hockey, my parents went to see a doctor, who informed them that my problem was partially due to the skates I was wearing and advised them to buy a custom-made pair. Dad and Mom decided on figure rather than hockey skates so I could take lessons—it was like the difference between day and night. I stepped out onto the ice with my new skates on and thought, Boy, this is easy. I loved it immediately. I was six and a half when I took my first figure skating lesson and was competing at the provincial level by the age of nine.

Every now and then when I am back in Seaforth, I run into that coach, who just shakes his head and says, "I can't believe where you got to . . . for someone who couldn't skate."

Isabelle

I began figure skating lessons with a group of ten other children. We had to go through a series of badges, and when you earned so many, you were allowed to take lessons with only two or three other kids. I was pretty lucky because I went through quickly. The president of the skating club allowed me to earn all my badges in a year and a half instead of the normal three.

At the end of that first year, we put on a show. I was asked to do a solo, which was unusual for a beginner. I was still only six. I remember I wore an orange outfit with a big hat that was made from a pizza box and covered with orange material. My mom made it and I thought I looked fantastic! I have to admit, however, that her costumes weren't always appreciated. Once, just after I began lessons, the kids in my group told me that since it would be Halloween the next time we skated, we should all dress up in costumes. Naively, I believed them, went home and told my mother, who insisted I dress up like a bunny, complete with a carrot. I arrived at the rink on Halloween in costume with a carrot in my hand, opened the door and saw the other skaters, who were dressed normally. They laughed at me and I was so embarrassed. I had to skate in that bunny outfit all night because I hadn't brought a change of clothes!

I began competing at the age of seven as a single and also with my brother in pairs. Dominique, who is three years older than I am, was really my first partner although we only skated together for about three months. He quit figure skating, preferring hockey instead. I can't remember too much about the actual competitions except that I finished last all the time. It wasn't until I met my new coaches, Eric Gillies and Josée Picard, that I began to do better at the competitions. Before I was taken on by them, I had two other teachers, who were provided by the club. As a skater moved up a level, he or she would change to another coach, which I did.

I was eight years old when my parents brought me to see Josée and Eric, who would stay with me throughout my career. It was their custom to take a couple of days to look at a skater and decide whether there was any potential and if they wanted to teach you. After the trial period, they informed me and my parents that I was to be accepted as a student, and not a month later I was teamed up with the boy who was to be my pairs partner until I met Lloyd.

Lloyd

I zoomed through the badges and all the little tests, loving every aspect of figure skating right from the start. Not only did I find it easy but I also enjoyed the social aspects of the sport. There were always several other people out on the ice, and since I loved to talk, I could start up a conversation any time I wanted to. In fact, I usually got into trouble for talking too much on the ice.

In a way, I suppose, I was and still am a bit of a contradiction because even though I enjoyed being with others there were many times when I preferred to just do my own thing. Figure skating provided me with that opportunity. I was never really much of a team player and often liked to be left alone. So, in skating, I could just go out there and zing around by myself, if I wanted. I didn't have to worry about anyone else.

Skaters usually begin by taking lessons with other children but my first coaches, Bruce and Fran Brady, taught individuals as well as groups and I took private lessons almost immediately. They were good people, especially Fran. I thought she was beautiful and I always liked to receive instruction from her. When they would ask,

"Who do you want your lessons from today?" I would answer, "Oh, Mrs. Brady please." I had quite a crush on her.

I remember my first solo. I had long hair, down to my shoulders, that hung over my eyes and ears. People would say, "Get that kid's hair cut." I loved my hair, which I thought looked great. But I wore a geeky-looking jumpsuit and people were laughing at me because I was trying to emulate Toller Cranston. He was fun to imitate and all of the kids tried to copy his moves. I wasn't at all shy or nervous when I got to center ice. I loved to be out there in front of all the people with everyone looking at me.

The first competition I won was an interpretative event. I was out on the ice, again imitating a well-known skater, and heard everybody saying, "Oh, he's so cute. Look at him out there." I was seven years old and beating people I shouldn't have. When I received that first trophy, I don't think there was a happier kid alive.

Fran and Bruce were typical small-town coaches. Fran had a knack for the artistic and theatrical side of skating while Bruce was more of a technician and workhorse. It was always, "Do it, do it, do it," from Bruce. He was a real disciplinarian. But they were friends of my parents, and because everyone was familiar with each other, I wasn't ever afraid to talk to my coaches. They also accompanied us to competitions, where they were in total charge.

One competition in particular stands out distinctly in my mind. I was eight years old and skating in Sarnia, Ontario, at the Western Ontario Section Winter Invitational Competition. My program was divided into three segments and I thought I was ready to go. I did the first part and then for some reason my mind went blank. I had no idea what was going on and after stumbling around a little bit, I began to cry. Totally humiliated, I started to get off the ice and Bruce, who was standing right there looking at me, said, "You get your ass back out there. Don't come off this ice until you're finished." Well, the music was still playing and people were probably wondering what I was doing. I had cried through the whole middle section, which lasted about a minute, and then the last part of the music came on and all of a sudden I knew what I was doing again. I finished the competition, got off and was disciplined. I placed second to last, eleventh out of twelve, if I remember correctly. It was awful. But, in the beginning, Bruce was like that, a total disciplinarian . . . just get the job done.

Isabelle

Josée and Eric were really great, and I loved them, but they were also very strict and demanded respect.

The arena where they taught was a forty-five minute drive from my house and in the beginning I would see them three times a week for fifteen-minute lessons. I was taught various things during this time and then I would go off by myself and practice what I had learned for the rest of the session.

I was a quiet and shy child and never got into serious trouble but I was still disciplined, along with the other children, whenever it was merited. Discipline usually came in the form of long, stern lectures by one of my coaches or my dad. If I wasn't concentrating or trying hard enough, they would team up at times and use various scare tactics, either threatening to stop me from skating or keeping me out of a competition. Sometimes they would compare me to others, asking, "Why can't you do it?" referring to a jump or a particular move. "See, she can do it and she's going to beat you if you can't." Dad would tell me there was no point in my continuing with skating if I couldn't get whatever jump it was that I was trying to master.

But all forms of discipline were verbal, not physical, unlike in some other schools. The closest I came to being physically disciplined was when I was taken by the shoulder and given a good shaking. If we were doing a stroking session, which is basic skating around the ice, they sometimes pushed us to move faster but that was more like a game. There was no doubt that Josée and Eric ran our lessons with a firm hand. I used to feel quite scared at times but always, as soon as we stepped out of the rink, my coaches became my friends.

Josée was like a second mother to me. She would take me shopping or bring me little gifts if she had been on vacation. Eric would play with the students after a session. They were like parents who would tell you to go and do your homework and when it was done you could have fun. My parents trusted them completely. Mom and Dad studied how they coached for a long time and saw that their techniques were working for me.

Josée and Eric also had the uncanny knack of knowing exactly which buttons to push. If I had had a difficult day at school or at home, or if I was depressed, they knew just what to say. Even today it is like that. Sometimes, if I have something on my mind, Josée will know exactly what I am thinking.

Right from the beginning we were taught that image was everything and Josée would be the one to comment on how I looked or acted. We had to be on our best behavior in public. Chewing gum was forbidden and we always had to dress well. My mother would give money to Josée, who would take me shopping. If she found something she thought was suitable, she would buy it for me. She would tell me how to wear my hair, how to sit and how to stand. I soon grew to seek her acceptance in all those aspects, and when I see Josée now, I am conscious of the fact that I still want that same approval.

I was never told to lose weight, thank goodness! But I recall both Josée and Eric being concerned whenever I dropped a couple of pounds. At those times, they would bombard me with questions such as, "What's wrong with you? Why are you so skinny? Did you go to the gym? Why are you weak?" I wasn't strong enough. I wasn't big enough. They would take me to the gym to work out and to restaurants to get me to eat.

My parents had a good friend we called Ti-Paul, which means Little Paul, who also had a daughter in skating. Because he was retired, he would drive us to lessons.

A month after I was accepted by Josée and Eric, they mentioned to Ti-Paul that they had a little boy student and wondered if my parents would mind if I skated with him. Everyone approved and that little boy, Pascal Courchesne, became my first and only pairs partner before Lloyd—aside from the brief time I skated with my brother. After Pascal and I teamed up, I began concentrating more on pairs.

Pascal was three years older than I and a lot like Lloyd in that he was outspoken. If he didn't want to do something, he wouldn't and was often in trouble. I liked skating with him right from the start. We had fun together but we also fought like cats and dogs, about everything. I recall us hitting and swearing and yelling at each other. He'd tease me about wearing braces and I was often reduced to tears. I suppose we acted like a typical brother and sister. It's funny, though, because my own brother and I never fought. Not once.

Because Pascal's family didn't live nearby, he stayed at our house for about two or three years and we continued our bickering at home and at school. But our big fights were on the ice when one of us didn't want to do something. Yet, for all the quarreling, we were very close and would sometimes team up against our coaches. If Josée and Eric were planning something for us that we didn't want to do, Pascal and I would close ranks and try to figure out how to get around it.

We were both small for our age and I suppose people thought we were cute together but, when I watch old videos, I think we weren't bad, considering our age and our size. We actually did lifts right from the beginning. At our first competition we came sixth out of fourteen, and that was an achievement since we had only been skating together for about two months.

Unfortunately, I didn't fare as well the next day when I competed as a single. Pascal and I were staying with some friends the night of that pairs competition and the adults went out for dinner, leaving my brother in charge. He had strict orders to get us to bed on time. Well, he fell asleep but we didn't. We started playing and jumping and putting ice in the bed, and when my parents returned at 11:30 we were still up. The next day, I wasn't in great shape and I came last again.

When I was about ten, Pascal and I were at the prenovice level, competing in fours at Nationals with the seniors. Fours is when you have two pair teams competing together at the same time on the ice. In the early 1980s, there were no rules and anything could go. Well, we completed the competition and received our first standing ovation. The four of us stood looking at each other, dumbstruck at all the applause.

A year later, our first national competition in the novice category was held in Montreal, where our families and friends all showed up to cheer us on. I did not expect to do well, since it was the first time we were competing at that level. We were the first to skate and amazed ourselves and everyone else by coming second overall, losing first place by the score of only one judge. Our parents threw a huge party that night and I was in heaven . . . maybe I could realize the dreams that were beginning to take shape in my mind.

Lloyd

After a couple of years in the old house, we moved again, this time to a smaller one with much more land. My father bought a horse for us kids and we always had other types of pets, especially dogs.

Our property line bordered on the edge of the public school and if I had gone straight to class, the way I was supposed to, it wouldn't have taken me more than a few minutes. Typically, however, I just couldn't seem to make it on time. I'd think, Oh, I'm fifteen minutes late; well, tough luck. It never bothered me. I would just get lost on the way there, forever being very curious as to what was going on around me and distracted by whatever captured my attention. I was always at least twenty or thirty minutes late and Mom was constantly getting calls from the principal, whose office was quickly becoming a second home to me.

I also got into a lot of fights and at least once a week I would be back in that principal's office. The confrontations were always over figure skating, which just wasn't done by boys in Seaforth back then. I think I was the only boy in my town doing it and figure skating is not playing hockey with the rest of the guys. It didn't matter where you lived. In those days, if a boy figure skated, everybody assumed he was gay. It was as if something was wrong with you . . . why didn't you play hockey?

I was also very little, only four foot ten, until I was fifteen years old, when I suddenly shot up fourteen inches. So I was small and the other kids picked on me a lot. They'd call me "sissy" and "faggot." I can't remember how many times I heard, "There's that little faggot again going to skate or missing school." I hated that they would call me names, so I would mouth right back and get into a fight. Often it would begin in class and spill into the hall or schoolyard. I was never one to back down, which is probably why I was expelled once for four days (it was the third time in a week that I had been caught fighting). But I was raised to stand up for what I believed in and I always did.

Never once did I think there was anything wrong with figure skating. I didn't think for a minute that maybe I shouldn't be doing this if they were going to call me names for the rest of my life. I loved what I was doing. I didn't feel any different from the others; *they* always just treated me differently. I look back now and assume some of it had to do with a little bit of jealousy because I was allowed out of class to skate or because I was getting some recognition.

Now and then, when I return to Seaforth, I run into some of those old classmates who used to call me names and they will ask, "Hey Lloyd, how are you doing? Remember when I called you a little faggot and we got into a fight?" We laugh about it now but as kids we didn't laugh—we fought.

My dad, who is quite masculine, was always very funny about my skating. I guess he was concerned that I wouldn't be straight. He would talk to me without ever mentioning it but I always got the feeling he was worried. When I was a little older and met other boys who figure skated, Dad didn't like me hanging around with them. It was okay with him if I figure skated but he didn't want me to become too friendly with any of the other boy skaters. Until I was twelve or thirteen, I didn't realize why he was so concerned. When I finally understood what he was on about, I used to laugh at him.

Looking back, I certainly took a lot of abuse and name-calling because of the figure skating. But I stuck with it.

Isabelle

As I began to take skating more seriously, my schedule soon set me apart from other friends and classmates who weren't involved in the sport. My lessons with Josée and Eric were on Tuesday, Friday and Sunday. So, during the week, I would go to school in the daytime and, if I had a skating lesson, I would get off about twenty minutes before everyone else.

Ti-Paul would pick up me and his daughter and, on the way to the rink, we would eat, get changed and put on our skates in the back of the car. Once we arrived at the arena, we would skate from about 5:00 to 9:30, and then we would get back into the car and do our homework, with only the little overhead light to read by.

On Sunday, I would skate from 7:30 in the morning until 1:00 and then visit my grandma, who lived close to the rink. Monday and Wednesday nights were devoted to off-ice training. At these sessions, my dad would make me practice jumps in the living room. I skated at other times during the week as well but in my own town, so at least we didn't have to drive. Saturday was usually the only day I had off.

I was lucky because I never had to go very far to train and my parents or Ti-Paul would always drive me. When I started to attend summer school, which was about a month in duration, my mother would come with me and we would stay in a campsite near the school. We did that for the first few summers, but when I was ten I was finally sent on my own. I hated being apart from my family. I would miss them so much. Even at school it was a problem. If I had to eat lunch by myself, I would often feel sick because I was so lonely for my family. I remember calling my mother a lot to come and pick me up.

When I had to leave and stay away a while for a competition or for summer school, I would sometimes dream that I was at home in my room. I would wake up and realize that I wasn't and would start to cry. It was hard.

Lloyd

I loved being away from home and thought it was great to get away from my parents and sisters. I was never homesick. When I was about eight and a half, Fran and Bruce were going to Brantford, Ontario, for the summer to coach. Brantford was well known back then for its skating and my coaches decided to take me and some other kids with them to a summer school that was run by Kerry Leitch and his wife, Barb. I was also there to try for my preliminary figure.

For our testing back then, we started with preliminary and then moved on to first and through to eighth. That is how we used to be categorized in order to compete. Things have changed drastically now, but when I started your preliminary figure was your first.

In a fifteen-minute test before three judges, I was on the ice by myself doing figure eights. There was no music, just dead silence. Because I didn't have anything appropriate to wear for my test, Mr. Leitch, who wasn't even my coach at the time, went out and bought me a white shirt to wear with my cords and a little red clip-on tie. I passed the preliminary and, because of this kindness to me, I immediately felt comfortable around him. Although he was quite well known as a coach and because of his large size, I guess many people deemed him to be a formidable man but I thought he was nice. I mean, he bought me a shirt and a tie and I passed the test. I still have that tie and wouldn't give it away for anything.

Mr. Leitch was also responsible for christening me with the nickname "Herbie," which I carry today. The nickname was inspired by my habit of pinching—let me explain. When I was little, kids used to pinch other kids between their thumb and index finger, a technique known as a "Purple Herbie." That summer in Brantford, I got into the habit of trying to pinch girls in places I shouldn't have. I guess it wasn't very nice but I was really small and the girls were all so big and to me they looked great. Every time they walked past me they would turn so I couldn't pinch them. After witnessing this a few times, Mr. Leitch started calling me Herbie and the name stuck. Even today my family call me Herb. It has never bothered me and in fact, when I was a kid, I thought it was kind of neat. Maybe that's why I love giving other people nicknames. Of course, my favorite is Isabelle's, who will always be "Fred" to me.

Isabelle

I continued going to public school in St-Jean but I found that the more I skated and left school early to get to the rink, the more I felt different from the rest of my classmates.

When I was in grade three, I had a teacher who was a fan of figure skating, unlike many of the other teachers, who questioned why I had to miss any school for a sport. That was hard on my parents, who found it difficult to explain to them. But this particular teacher had a skating calendar hanging up in the classroom that depicted various skaters and coaches. One day I was standing at the front of a line while waiting to go outside and I was looking at the calendar. My teacher was there and we began talking about figure skating. I pointed to the calendar and said, "One day I will be in there," and the other kids, hearing this, looked at me as if I was weird. I emphatically restated, "No, I will be!" I hadn't met Josée and Eric yet as this happened just before I started lessons with them. Eric's picture was included in the calendar and I continued to amuse my classmates and teacher by saying, "One day I would like one of them to be my coach." A few weeks later, my dad came home and said, "We have found new coaches for you," and of course they were Josée and Eric.

Gradually, my friends became the people I skated with because I was around them all the time. I think, in a way, that is why I continued to skate, because I did make so many friends in the sport. If things weren't going well for me at the rink, I was at least content with the knowledge that I would be with my friends. I knew they would understand.

Although I studied ballet and jazz, my lessons were sporadic. I would take classes for a season and then stop for a few years and then start again in different classes. I also tried soccer for a couple of summers but soon grew to hate it. I was the only girl on the team and the reason I didn't quit was that my parents repeatedly told me to finish whatever I started. I finished the season and I never went back.

Lloyd

When I was nine years old, Bruce and Fran told me that, if I wanted to improve in the sport, I was going to have to train with someone else. They suggested Kerry and Barb Leitch's school, which was in the Cambridge area, but thought I should first try Mr. Leitch's summer school in Kitchener.

Today, Kerry Leitch is known to skaters as a god among coaches and is considered to be one of the top three in the world. Even at that time, many of his skaters were competing at the national level. As soon as I saw him that summer, he said, "Oh, Herbie is back." I felt comfortable right away even though I was the smallest kid at the school and knew no one.

In the beginning, it was much harder than skating at Seaforth, where I had skated only two or three days a week (ice time was scarce because minor hockey leagues controlled the rinks). At home, I usually skated an hour in the morning and an hour or two after school. Although I took most of my tests and badges in Seaforth, and practiced there a lot, my training was not so regimented. Mind you, in the summer, wherever I was, I skated all day long.

I got along well with Mr. Leitch. Although he had skated some singles and, I believe, went on to become a junior national competitor, in my eyes he was really something because he had also played baseball in the minor leagues and had signed with a professional team. I remember playing ball with him and being amazed at how fast he could throw. Because of his pro ball history, the size of his school and, probably most importantly, the fact that he had bought me that tie the year before, I decided to stay on.

That summer, I was introduced to pairs skating and a little girl by the name of Lorri Baier. Before then, I had only skated singles. They put Lorri and I together and told us to skate. Well, at that time, I didn't like holding hands and neither did she. We absolutely refused so Mr. Leitch skated with us around the rink, holding our hands together. We both hated it . . . oh no, he's a boy, she's a girl. But we ended up skating together from that day until April 1982.

I continued to skate both singles and pairs. Mr. Leitch was adamant that we do both. I remember competing in Toronto at the end of every summer and being entered in pairs, singles and the interpretative event. They used to give out little plaques to winners and I probably have fifty of them. I was always competing against people who were much older than I was and I was beating them either as a single or with Lorri. My podium pictures at these events are really quite funny: the other guys, who placed either second or third, were eighteen or nineteen years old and towered over me. There are also several of Lorri and I on the podium; we are the little ones on top.

Not long after Lorri and I began skating together, we competed at the sectional level in prejuvenile pairs and won. All Lorri and I did was shadow skate, which is when you skate beside each other, doing the same thing; we weren't big enough to perform lifts and throws. To compensate for our size, Mr. Leitch had to be innovative and come up with some cutesy moves. We would attempt little lifts and people would laugh hysterically. (Lorri and I were exactly the same height and weight and we grew together until we were fourteen or fifteen.) When I think about it now, we probably won because we were so cute, not because we were better than the other pairs. It may not have been the right way to win but it certainly fueled the fire and made us persevere, trying to improve.

After the prejuvenile win, we continued with small competitions and the next year we competed juvenile and then prenovice.

My partner was from Mitchell, so my mother and Lorri's mother, Donna, would take turns driving us to Cambridge every day during the winter. Mom would take me out of school an hour early because we had to be in Mitchell by 3:15 to start at 4:00 in Cambridge. Lorri's sister, Sherri, was also taking classes with us, so the three of us would be driven to the rink. We skated until 7:00 and then would be driven back to Mitchell by 8:15 p.m. If Donna drove, one of my parents would be in Mitchell waiting to drive me home. I did all my homework in the car and ate my dinner there as well. My mom says she lived in our old station wagon during this time. We made this trip on Monday, Tuesday, Wednesday and on Saturday, when we would skate from 6:00 p.m. to midnight. We often weren't home until 2:00 in the morning and much of this driving was done in typical Ontario winters with snow, sleet and icy roads.

Kerry Leitch was the innovator of off-ice training in figure skating. He had us running stairs, lifting weights and laboring with chin-ups and push-ups after many of the sessions. Sometimes we wouldn't get home until 9:30 or 10:00 p.m. during the week. Six or seven hours of driving and skating, four days a week, is hard for people to imagine. For the longest time we didn't skate on Thursday, Friday or Sunday because it was too far to drive and because the ice was available only at 6:00 in the morning on those days. During these off-times, I would skate in Seaforth and Lorri would skate in Mitchell.

Although we were starting to do well, we decided not to lose the rest of our lives in the process. I continued to participate in other sports including golf, baseball, soccer and volleyball. In fact, I attempted to get involved in every type of sport. Lorri was just the opposite. She was more studious and intellectual, and preferred to read. We were definitely not at the point where we thought figure skating was going to be our career but we continued to skate and compete, constantly driving to and from the rink.

Isabelle

I'm not sure what motivated me to stay in figure skating. It became a drug, I think . . . almost addictive. You work hard because your parents tell you to always work hard and finish what you started and then you do well at a competition and you say, "That's cool, I want more." And so you work harder and harder and then you make it to the next level and do well and then the next. You grow up without really noticing it. It has a lot to do with the recognition; without it, I probably wouldn't have stuck it out.

My coaches would use every technique to try to pull out of me that little extra that I needed to give. They would use money, weekends away or gifts to motivate me to try even harder. They would tell me, for example, that I would have five chances to land a jump and, if I succeeded, they would pay me five, ten or twenty dollars. Each year, the amount of money increased. I recall being at a seminar with an American coach and having a difficult time with a jump. He placed his wallet on the boards and told me that if I landed it I could have whatever amount of money was in the wallet. I asked him, "What if there is only a penny in there?" and he replied that that was the chance I would have to take. I tried so hard to land that jump but just couldn't manage it on that day, although I came close. It turned out that there was $120 in the wallet. But the point of this exercise was that I practiced the jump so much that I landed it shortly thereafter.

My dad would also try to bribe me. I had always wanted a dog and he told me if I was able to make two jumps that I had been having trouble with, he would buy me one. It took me a year and I not only perfected the jumps but many other moves as well. Dad bought me the dog.

My mother was more relaxed about my competitions, and my skating in general. She supported me but, if I missed a jump, she wouldn't say anything. Mom was at the rink once when I was practicing a solo. It was a really cute number. I had to perform this little wiggly thing with my rear end but I was very shy about it. The routine was such that I would have to skate full speed and then do the wiggly thing, then turn around and do a jump. I think I did that solo about twenty times that night. Either my skating or positioning was wrong or my little wiggly thing wasn't good enough or I missed my jump. I cried from the first run-through to the last and came off the ice with tears streaming down my face. Mom loved skating and wanted me to succeed in the sport but she didn't like how it affected me emotionally. She was very concerned and said in her gentle way, "I hate to see you cry." I replied, "Oh, it's okay. Do you think I'll land my jump at the competition?" It didn't matter to me that I was crying; my only concern was how I skated.

My dad, on the other hand, was a little bit different. He was what we call a "skating dad." In comparison, if he had watched my terrible practice, he would have asked, "What was your problem? Why couldn't you just do it the first or second time? If you had done it at the start you wouldn't have had to do it twenty times. You are wasting your time. Do you get that?"

When I was about eight years old, I had been working on one particular jump that I just couldn't seem to land in front of my father. Dad kept saying that I couldn't do it. At that time, I was living away from home during the week, staying with a family, and he made a point of coming to the rink whenever he could to watch me. When he was there I was so nervous that I would miss the jump. One night, after he had seen me fall, he said to my coach, "See, she can't do the jump." My coach told him that I could do it but only when he (my father) wasn't around. Well, I had been picked to compete the following weekend and so my dad brought a video camera and said, "Okay, she has three of these jumps in her competition and now I'm going to videotape her routine. If she misses the three of them and I have it on tape, she is not competing this weekend."

My coach started the music and, as my dad videotaped from the boards, I fell once, twice, then three times. Dad was really angry and decided to leave the rink. As he did, he said, "See, I knew I came for a reason. I knew it. Friday night, I am coming to pick you up and you are going home, because I have it on video! I have the proof that you can't do that jump!"

I cried so much when he told me I couldn't compete. Looking back on this, I realize his attitude forced me to work even harder. In a way, it also taught me how to handle the pressure during competition. No judge could make me as nervous as my dad. Although it was tough on me as a child, I have no regrets that he pushed me the way he did, teaching me to finish whatever I started. I carry that discipline with me today.

Dad eventually gave in and let me compete that weekend and I didn't find out why until many years later. Apparently, there was no film in the camera and he hadn't realized it. He had no proof. So he let me compete and I made all three jumps and won the competition!

Lloyd

My dad never put any kind of pressure on me to skate well. He was laid back about it and always told me that if I didn't want to skate at any time, I didn't have to. Both my parents told me that if skating ever stopped being fun and I wasn't enjoying it, then I shouldn't do it.

Although my mother was never a "skating mom," she did take my sport very seriously. It was: "He did that, he is no good. He did poorly at this competition; he's never going to make it. Get him out of there." But my dad would reply, "Just relax and let him do what he wants to do."

Mom was at the rink all the time but only because she had to drive me there. She would stay, chatting it up with the other mothers, and would sit in the stands, knitting or doing paperwork. She was never the type of parent, like some others, who would hang over the boards and think they were coaches. Mr. Leitch, for one, wouldn't allow that and for a long time didn't even let parents in the arena.

Dad never went to the rink. I would ask him if he wanted to come and he would say, "Well, the garden needs work. Maybe next time." Not that he was never there to support me. It's just that he wasn't a "skating dad" who felt he had to watch me all the time.

Because I was away a lot, Mr. Leitch became a second parent to me. He never really intruded on my personal life but would set the rules when I was away from home at competitions or at summer school. He took me under his wing because I was a hell-raiser. I used to get into trouble for swearing at the older kids, who constantly picked on me because of my size. They would say, "Oh, there's little Herbie," and I would lip off to them because I wasn't afraid, even though I was ten and most of these guys were seventeen or eighteen.

I also used to mouth back at my coaches and Mr. Leitch was a firm believer that if another person is older than you, you must treat them with respect, whether it be coaches or other skaters. That is why to this day I refer to Kerry Leitch as Mister. It was bred into us as kids. You used a title for everyone who was older and never called them by their first name. I grew up to hate that and now, if I am introduced to someone, I will always ask if I can call them by their given name, but not Mr. Leitch. If I saw him on the street tomorrow, I could never say, "Hi, Kerry. How are you doing?" It would always be, "Hello, Mr. Leitch." I was never intimidated by him as a child and I am not now; I just wouldn't be comfortable addressing him in any other way.

So I would catch hell for not showing the proper respect to my elders and I would always try to weasel my way out of it . . . I wasn't wrong or I didn't say that or I didn't do it or you misinterpreted me. But I was forever getting caught by Mr. Leitch and I'd think, Goddamn, how did he catch me again? and I'd try to cover it another way the next time and I would get caught again.

I also liked to skip lessons and was often late, playing outside. I was a bit of a lazy student as well and would love to chat in the corner. One of my coaches would tell me to go and do something and I'd go out and do it and think, Oh gee, that was easy. If I can do that, then I don't have to work so hard. So I wouldn't concentrate and would often get kicked off sessions.

Mr. Leitch was a very hard disciplinarian. If I got into trouble, I would either receive a lecture or was made to stand at the side of the boards, and at times I was even slapped across the face or smacked on the butt with a skate guard. I suppose it was no different from getting the strap in the principal's office at school. My parents were aware of what was happening because I would always tell them and they would ask me if I deserved the punishment. After a while of thinking about it, I would state that I probably did and they would advise me that I would have gotten the same thing at home.

I was caught drinking a couple of times and can well remember the first time I had too much to drink. I was eleven years old and in Lake Placid for a seminar with all the other kids from the school. Most of the other students were much older than I was and thought it would be cool to serve little Herbie some beer. I was sick the next day but the other guys covered for me, telling Mr. Leitch I had the flu. If my coach knew about it, he never said anything. Maybe he thought I had learned a lesson on my own. The times he did catch me sneaking a beer, I was disciplined for it.

I never considered any punishment I received to be abuse. I needed to be disciplined. I was just that type of kid. If it wasn't for Mr. Leitch and his strict ways, I know I would not be where I am today. My parents always trusted him but many schools took a dim view of his authoritarian methods. Yet, he was the one who was getting results. Something had to be working.

He also had an extremely rigid dress code. You couldn't wear jeans to the rink. Well, if you didn't wear jeans at my school, you would really stand out. I had been teased enough about figure skating and I wasn't about to be harassed about the way I dressed as well, so I wore jeans and a T-shirt every day. This meant that, after school, I'd have to change in the car on the way to the rink or, once there, sneak into the bathroom and change quickly before Mr. Leitch caught me. Many times he would be waiting by the front door and would say, "You have your jeans on. You can't come in." Unbelievable! Some of us would wear pants over our jeans, but we always got caught.

So it was a constant battle between living in this small town and trying to please Mr. Leitch, who wanted me to mature and develop a more professional attitude toward figure skating. It was always drilled into us that impression is everything . . . that we had to look the part. I was never that way and I am still not today.

Isabelle

I think it cost my parents about $20,000 a year to finance my skating but it wasn't something we ever talked about. I never heard them say that I couldn't skate because they didn't have enough money.

Dad had his own company and Mom worked as his secretary and I don't believe we were ever deprived of anything. At Christmas, we always received a great gift that we wanted and during the rest of the year we had pretty much what we asked for. But we were brought up to be cautious with money too. For example, if I wanted a new outfit, I might have been told that I had to wait a couple of weeks but if it was something I really needed, I would usually get it right away.

My parents never said, though, that they couldn't buy Dominique or me something because the money had to go toward a new pair of skates. I couldn't imagine getting that kind of pressure. I was putting enough on myself as it was.

Lloyd

Almost everything was spent on skating and I learned very quickly how much it cost. When I was ten years old it took about $15,000 a year. That was a lot of money then and explains why both of my parents had to work. As soon as I was old enough, my dad hired me to work at his restaurants to help pay for skating as well.

My parents spent as much as they could afford on my sport without having to deprive anyone else in the family. When I was young, my father would labor for eighteen or nineteen hours a day to pay for skating and also, as he freely admits, because he loved to work. I think, had I not skated, that we could have been well-off. But they did everything to make it possible for me to skate because that was what I wanted to do and they supported me one hundred percent.

If I didn't feel like taking a lesson or practicing, my parents never pushed me to go to the rink or threatened to stop paying for it. I loved to play road hockey after school with the other kids and on occasion I would lie to my mother, telling her I was sick and not up to skating that day. I would wait a while, until I knew it was too late to get to the rink on time, and then recover miraculously and say, "You know what, Ma? I feel better. I think I'll play road hockey." I always figured that if I didn't want to do something, there was a way out of it. But even at those times, when I am sure my mom must have known what was going on, she didn't push me. I got into more trouble at home by not doing my chores than by not skating if I didn't feel like it. Both my parents were great about just letting me be. I think they realized that I got into enough hassles at the rink and at school without getting into them at home as well.

Isabelle

Aside from the expense, my figure skating took up a lot of my parents' time. I suspect it may have taken something away from my brother, although he says it didn't. I hope that is true.

My parents always tried to give us the same things and devote an equal amount of time to Dominique and me, but as I began to skate more, the time aspect was difficult. I believe my parents always treated us the same way. I want to think so. Dominique wished to go to university and I wanted to skate and we both respected that. My brother says he is happy for me and is content with his own life. He is an engineer now and is opening a rink and training center for skating. My mom, Lloyd and I are helping him.

Dominique knows how hard my life was at times and the sacrifices that I had to make. He has always been so supportive of my career because he knows how much work I had to put into it. He saw me cry. He also knows how difficult it was and is for me to travel all the time and be away from my family. I still get homesick. But I like to believe he is happy with both our choices and it made me feel good to hear him say, "I would never have had an Olympic experience if it hadn't been for you." It's nice to be able to give him something back for all the times he was there for me.

Lloyd

My parents always tried as much as they could to give everybody everything they wanted. I don't think my sister Marie suffered at all from my skating and I believe this was partially due to her being five years older. But she and I have always been able to talk openly and are the best of friends. She leads a busy and fulfilling life outside Seattle. Besides being married and looking after her two children, she also works at a bank and is a part-time trainer of Morgan horses.

Unfortunately, my little sister, Mary Jane, may not have had as much of my parents' time as she wanted and she tended to be very jealous of my skating. She is a school teacher in Tennessee and is more comfortable with her own life now, but when we were kids she was always searching for her own niche. I remember her trying skating, piano and singing, among other things. But because she couldn't seem to find what she did best, she would get upset at me. We have talked about her feelings since we've grown up and she admits that she felt slighted because I was the skater and, in her eyes, the popular one. I never looked at it like that or thought about it in that way. To me, family is family and no member is any better than the others. I think she finally realizes all the hard work I had to put into my career and I'm just glad we've reached a point in our lives where we can talk about it.

Isabelle

Sometimes I look at a young person who is beginning to skate and I think, You don't know what you are getting into. I want to say, Get out while you can, before you get addicted. Yet I would also be the first one out there to help, if I could.

When I was a child, skating was fun; it is still fun today. But there was also tremendous pressure, most of which I put on myself. I always wanted to skate well, and if I had a bad skate I would be very negative toward any mistakes that I made. I was forever asking myself, Why did you do that? Why did you fall? I suppose in a way that was good because, whatever I attempt now, I always give one hundred percent. But if I had it to do over again I would try to do it with less crying and be less critical of myself.

Aside from the internal pressure, skating at the competitive level is a pressure cooker on its own. You are not only competing against others but are being judged as well, and that is hard on a child who was as sensitive as I was. I would train to the point of exhaustion and then have it all come down to two minutes out on the ice, and if I fell, which I did a lot in the beginning, I was never easy on myself.

And then there are the sacrifices. If I wanted to see results, I had to skate every day whether I felt like it or not. I had to work every day whether I wanted to or not. My friends who weren't in the sport would be outside playing while I was inside skating. It always came first.

But with all the pressure and sacrifices, there were also the moments when the pure joy of skating made it worthwhile. If it didn't balance itself out, I don't think I could have done it.

Lloyd

Like most kids, I never had a great attention span but I did have a huge amount of self-esteem and confidence. Whenever I won or received a medal, I thought it was great and would think, Look at me, I'm good! That probably motivated me more than anything. It came from inside rather than from someone else telling me I had to win.

I loved to compete, and even if I didn't come first I always thought that I should have. I would ask myself why I didn't. But then I would go back and work harder or change something and tell myself that next time I was going to win. Very seldom was I not in the top three on the podium and I think it was because I had such a compelling drive to be number one. It's almost addictive. You win once and you want to win again, and the more you win, the more you want to win. It's the recognition too. I always liked it when people came up to me and said, "Hey, you are really good."

But I don't believe most kids have that kind of self-esteem at such an early age. It's hard on children, being in a competitive sport where you are judged all the time and having to accept someone else's decision as the final one. From that standpoint, it is really difficult for a child to look forward and always see the bright side of the sport. You have to be tough.

CHAPTER TWO

Growing Up Different

Lloyd

I DIDN'T HAVE a lot of friends in high school. When I started grade nine in 1977, some of the older kids were still hassling me and calling me the usual names. But by then I was competing at the national level and trying very hard to live up to Mr. Leitch's dictum regarding our image and so I more or less let the teasing slide. Occasionally my temper would get the better of me and I would reply in kind, but for the most part I chose to ignore it.

I think part of the problem was that I was away so much. Lorri and I had won the novice pairs national championship earlier that year and, by the time I started high school, we were on our way to the Junior Worlds in France. Although I was getting a little recognition for our accomplishments at this time, it certainly didn't come from my classmates. My peers seemed to take little interest in figure skating and I didn't blame them. I mean, who at the age of thirteen or fourteen will actually sit down and watch it on television unless they are really into the sport? Some of their parents were fans and they were the ones noticing our rise.

My figure skating prevented me from being part of the "in"

crowd in high school. In fact, I was an outcast and the few good friends I made fell into that category as well. My best friend was Pam Carnochan and, to this day, we are very close. Pam helped me all the time. Whenever I was away she would photocopy any school notes and mail them to me or have them ready when I came back. If I prepared an assignment while I was out of town, I could send it to her and she would make sure it was turned in. She even wrote a couple of essays for me and signed my name. Without Pam, I don't think I would have made it through high school.

Although skating always came first, I managed to be part of every sporting team in school. I played badminton, soccer and volleyball and was on the golf team for five consecutive years and seemed to excel at everything. The badminton team made the all-Ontario finals five years in a row. In golf, we were the all-Ontario champions during my fourth year of high school, when I also won low gross. I was one of the better players on all the teams but still couldn't seem to be accepted by that elite crowd. People just wouldn't talk to me. It was like: Oh, there is the skater. He is probably missing another class today. I believe most people thought one day I would grow out of my obsession. I look back now and think the whole situation was probably just as much my fault as theirs. They didn't speak to me and I didn't go out of my way to talk to them because I just thought, Well, what is the sense? I am going to be away and they don't really want to include me in anything anyway. I was definitely being ostracized but I was too busy to really let it bother me.

Seaforth continued to be my home throughout my high school years. When I was thirteen, we moved again to a house my dad built. It was on a piece of property that Mom's father had owned and consisted of almost an acre of lawn in the back, a pool and a big two-car garage. I loved that house because I got to live in the basement, away from my parents and sisters. The whole area had been converted to a large bedroom with its own entrance and it was perfect because I was able to come and go as I pleased.

Just before I began high school, Mr. Leitch suggested that Lorri and I go to school in Preston. A lot of kids who skated at the club had moved to the area and he thought living there would allow us to get the extra ice time. But I was adamant about staying in Seaforth. Not only was it familiar to me but the school was much smaller. I knew, with the number of classes I could be missing, I'd be able to receive special attention in Seaforth as opposed to a larger place, where I might get lost in the shuffle. Lorri felt the same way about Mitchell and our parents completely supported us. Although we got into a big row with Mr. Leitch over our decision, we stuck to our guns and won out.

Choosing not to move, however, meant continuing with the grueling drive back and forth to Preston. On Monday, Tuesday and Wednesday, I left school at 2:00, missing the last two classes. Once we arrived at the rink, we would skate from 4:00 to 7:15 and then drive back home. On Thursday and Friday, I would be at school all day but on Saturdays I skated another six hours back in Preston. Those were regular sessions, where homework would still be done in the car and usually handed in at the last possible moment. But, prior to every competition, we would actually move to Preston for two weeks, board with various families and skate and train vigorously almost all day. Obviously, I would have to miss school during these periods but Pam or my parents would mail my work to me, and when I returned home, I would have to catch up on the weekends.

But even with all the school I missed, I found the work to be quite simple. I never could understand how kids could fail or fall behind. I mean, I was away so much with my skating, and as I grew older, I would sometimes skip class and just say I went skating, although I was actually at the beach or somewhere else having a good time. The teachers didn't question me because they were used to my not being there. I never strived to be an A student, though. I guess if I had concentrated on that, maybe I would have had problems. But a B is what I aimed for. I look back now and consider myself fortunate that high school was so easy for me. Many of the other kids were still treating me differently and the constant demands of training and skating took up most of my time and energy. I imagine the pressure would have been much greater if I had found school to be difficult on top of everything else I had to contend with.

Isabelle

By the time I was twelve, I was spending so many hours skating, I wasn't able to attend regular school. Instead, Pascal and I were being tutored at home in the evenings. Every morning, my brother would drive us to the rink where we would train from about 7:30 to 2:00. Pascal and I would then take the bus back and, after a fifteen-minute walk from the station, we usually arrived home by 4:00. Our classes began at 4:30 and continued until 6:30 and during this time we constantly teased each other. If one of us answered incorrectly, the other would immediately bestow the proper punishment by throwing an eraser directly at his or her head. Despite the fighting, we managed to pay attention and get through the classes. We had to because, although we were being tutored privately, all our exams were taken at school. After dinner, there was either homework or off-ice training. We did this every day for two years, Monday through Friday, with only the weekends off.

By 1983, we had begun competing at the national level and the Quebec team usually traveled by bus to the city where the event was to be held. Most of the time, I was the youngest on the team and, apart from that, I was certainly the smallest. When I was twelve the other kids were about seventeen, and they used to like to party and have fun on our trips. While they played music on the bus, all I wanted to do was sleep. I would gather some jackets, curl up on top of the luggage racks and settle in for a long nap.

At the age of fourteen, I changed training centers and went to Boucherville, where Lloyd and I still train. There were nine of us skating full time, which was really a rare situation. My dad wanted me to have a formal education, and when he saw how many of us were in the same boat, he developed what I think was a terrific idea. There was a high school beside the rink, and after discussing his plans with the rink manager, the two of them approached the school to suggest a program in which we could skate for half the day and go to school for the other half. Out of this, "Study and Sport" was born, which still exists today in Boucherville.

All of the skaters took classes together, apart from the other students. Although it was great to finally be in regulated sessions, there were some problems attached to it that evolved out of the closeness of the group. Everybody knew about each other's lives. Pascal and I were already receiving some recognition, having placed second at the 1983 Novice Nationals in Montreal. By 1984, we were competing at the Junior Nationals, where we placed fifth. Because we skated with our classmates for half the day and then spent the other half in school with them, they would all know whether we had a bad skate at a competition or just a bad day at the rink. They also knew if I fought with my partner or coaches, so it was difficult to attend and just be a regular student. The kids in school who weren't skaters couldn't understand why we were so involved in the sport, and because I felt different from them, I spent most of my free time with the other skaters as well.

I finished high school in the Study and Sport Program with good grades. I always did fine in school. I was very disciplined: skating helped me to become that way. Yet, although I was the type to always get the job done, I definitely needed a goal to motivate me. If I had a week to do homework and, say, it was given to me on a Monday morning, I wouldn't do it until 10:30 the following Sunday night. I just can't work if I don't see the goal and I am the same way with skating. That is why my coaches were always entering me into competitions whenever they could. Summertime was the worst for me—no competitions, so why work? I am still like that today. I perform much better when working towards a goal.

Lloyd

Lorri and I, quickly climbing the ranks together, developed a brother-sister type of relationship. In the beginning, we didn't like each other much and fought all the time because we never had the same ideas when it came to skating. But, as the partnership evolved, Lorri took control. She would determine how our practice sessions would be run and decided everything from what we would wear to what we would work on each day.

We had a fantastic career as a pairs team. I remember in 1977, when we were both fourteen, we won the novice Canadian pairs championship. We were the first team in our category ever to do a throw double Axel. That was because we couldn't lift. I weighed eighty-four pounds and Lorri weighed eighty-two and we were both four foot ten. We managed only one overhead lift but we did two throws and everyone said, "Wow, look at these little kids doing this big throw!"

That was the year I met Brian Orser, who won the novice men's national championship. Aside from meeting Brian, one other incident from that competition stands out in my mind. Novice pairs followed the senior dance and the dancers had already completed one section of their program. We were all going into the dressing room at the same time, and as I walked in and realized who was there, I thought, Oh my God, these are the guys who are going to the Worlds . . . the bigwigs. There was Rob McCall, Randy Burk, Greg Young and David Martin and here I was, a little wee guy, just starting out. I sat down by myself and no one said a word to me. They were joking around and laughing hysterically and I remember sitting there, quiet as a mouse, listening intently to their animated conversation.

Over the next little while I got to know Rob and his partner, Marie McNeil, very well. They were competing at Skate Canada, where Lorri and I had been invited to do exhibitions because, at that time, there was no pairs competition at the event; it was strictly dance and singles. From that point on, Rob and Marie and I hit it off. By then I also knew Brian Orser quite well. Brian and Rob were wonderful friends and we all got along great. I remember thinking that Marie, without a doubt, had her act together and she was definitely in control of that team. Rob was the wild one but he was incredibly talented. He loved life very much and never missed an opportunity to enjoy it.

After winning novice, Lorri and I were on our way to the Junior

Worlds in France, where we came in sixth out of seven competitors. We were so young and still quite small. That was the year when Barbara Underhill and Paul Martini won in our category. Barb and Lorri were exactly the same age, born on the same day, and Paul was a little older and bigger than I. We were to compete against Barb and Paul in many more competitions over the ensuing years. Brian was also on that team. He came in fourth, Brian Boitano placed third and Dennis Coi, God rest his soul, became the junior world champion. Tracey Wainman was also there. It was a "Who's Who" of teams.

As I was growing up, I met many world-class skaters but I never considered any of them to be my mentor. Some of the older guys at the club took me under their wing and guided me along. Although they were very helpful, for some reason I never wanted to emulate them, other than hoping that one day I would be able to do lifts. I never thought, Oh, I want to be like him. I believed that I was the greatest thing out there.

The only sports figure who came close to being a hero to me when I was young was tennis player John McEnroe. Let the talent speak for itself is what he personified to me and I believe that today. Who cares what people think of you as a person? You should be able to speak your mind, regardless of the outcome. I admired John's competitive drive, how he always wanted to win and how he always gave one hundred percent. I was somewhat rebellious myself and to see John talk back to the umpires and question their authority . . . well, I understood where he was coming from.

As teenagers on the competitive circuit, our training at Mr. Leitch's school continued to be very tough. Expectations were high and it was a lot of hard work. I think it was more difficult for the girls than for the boys. Mr. Leitch never showed any favoritism and the training, lectures and expectations were the same for all of us. In those days, I don't believe most young girls were as prepared for that as the boys were and I think they probably should have been treated with a gentler hand.

Our off-ice training included weight and circuit training and stair running. Every Friday, we ran five miles. On the ice, we did three short and two long programs every day. Mr. Leitch believed physical training led to improvement. I hated it and every time I expressed my thoughts, I would be disciplined and wound up doing far more work than if I had kept quiet. I recall running stairs for three hours at a time on various occasions. But no matter what the discipline, it didn't stop me from questioning the rules.

Hockey, the sport that began it all for me, suddenly attracted my interest again when I was about fifteen. I could skate circles around everybody—a far cry from the kid who had tried out for the team nine years earlier. I wasn't very good at puck handling because I didn't grow up with it. But I could outskate anybody and the other kids would always want me on their team. I love hockey and still play in the senior league in Montreal. We are three-time city champions.

Before I turned sixteen, I grew well over a foot and was suddenly all arms and legs. I couldn't do a thing. I just sprouted up and, because of the rapid growth, I lost all my jumps. It altered my body but, more importantly, it changed our skating. It was at that point that Lorri and I could begin to do more difficult things and we went on to become junior national pairs champions and junior world bronze and silver medalists.

Because skating was taking up so much of my life as a teenager, there wasn't much time or opportunity for the usual pursuits and pleasures of someone my age. I didn't go out on a date, for instance, until I was in grade eleven when I asked Pam if she would like to go to the prom with me. It was just awful. We had been friends for so long and had not thought of each other in a romantic way before. We argued and fought the whole night and our entire dating relationship only lasted a couple of weeks, until we decided to go back to being just good friends. When I did find the time to date, though, it was usually with girls I knew from skating.

I continued skating singles as well as pairs throughout this period and, in 1980, I surprised everyone by becoming novice national Canadian men's champion. At that point, I decided to quit singles to concentrate solely on pairs. I only used to do it because I thought it was fun and easy and found it to be a great tension release, but I never really believed I would make anything of it.

That same year Lorri and I competed for the first time as a senior pair at Nationals and we were thrilled to come second in that category. Everybody else thought we should have won and continued on to Senior Worlds but that wasn't destined to happen until 1982, when we finally competed at that much-aspired-to level.

The Senior World Championships were being held in Copenhagen, Denmark, and Lorri and I were in awe of being at such an event. The competition was in March and I had broken my wrist during a fall, six months earlier. Various doctors wanted to do a bone graft and had put several casts on it but it wasn't healing properly. The powers that be were going to pull me out of the National and World championships but I refused to let them do that. Instead, I requested a cast be made that would allow me to do the lifts. So they fitted my arm with something called a cutter cast, which was made from fiberglass. It was put on in such a position that I could perform the lifts. Lorri learned to hang on to me when I couldn't hold on to her. Right before the World Championships, I was due to get a new cast but was apprehensive since it always took me a while to get used to it. I recall standing there, ready to go on the ice at the championship competition, and looking down to see blood dripping out of my cast. Apparently, it had rubbed my hand raw inside. We stuffed it to stop the bleeding and Lorri and I competed with my arm in that condition for two days. Because the cast was so irritating, I couldn't wait to get it off. So, after the event was over, an American doctor tried to cut the plaster, using a normal pair of scissors. It took hours and I was so annoyed by it all that I never did put it back on. My wrist bone healed just fine on its own and we placed eighth at the Senior Worlds.

Isabelle

Pascal and I skated through all the early levels together and in 1984 we were asked to compete in what would be our first international experience, at the Coupe des Alpes. That competition stands out in my mind because it was the first time I traveled so far from home. It was also the longest time I was away.

I was thirteen years old and the two-week competition was held in France, for one week, and Germany, for the other. I was rooming with an English girl and, because I didn't speak the language myself, I was miserable. The rest of the team spoke English. I really wished someone from my family had been able to come. Thank goodness my coach Josée was there. She continued to travel with me to most of my competitions and had a way of making me feel more at ease. I think that is part of the reason why we remain good friends today.

We skated well in France, placing fifth, but I remember traveling on the train to Germany and my mind playing tricks on me. I thought, I am going home now . . . I am going home. But no, I had one more week to go. I recall waking up in Germany after dreaming I was in my own room at home again. I used to do that a lot. I could actually see my bedroom furniture. When I opened my eyes, I started to cry. I was missing home so much. We came fifth in Germany as well, so the skating wasn't a problem. It was me and my feelings of homesickness. There were so many new things to see and experience but I only wished my parents were there to see them with me.

In December of that year, we went to Junior Worlds in Colorado. We were going to be away for three weeks, and before we left for the airport, I tried so hard not to cry. My dad, my mom, my brother and his girlfriend (now his wife) drove me to the airport and I kept thinking, I don't want to leave. We had to be in Colorado early to get used to the high altitude and, for the first few days, no one else was there, except the team leader. Training for the competition was hard. Pascal's nose kept bleeding and I was very tired for the whole time but I knew the reason we had come so early was to get accustomed to all that.

Most of the young people were speaking English again and I found myself really lonely. Although Pascal is French, he could speak some English and wasn't shy at all. He was a lot like Lloyd and found it easy to mix with people. But I didn't speak the language and I was so shy and homesick.

Every evening I went for a walk. It snowed all the time but it wasn't very cold and the surrounding landscape looked like a fairy tale to me . . . the lights and the snow. I didn't have to wear my toque and I couldn't believe it. I was amazed that it was snowing and yet I didn't have to wear my hat . . . not at all like our Canadian winters. It was so beautiful.

In Broadmoor, where our competition was being held, we stayed at a lovely hotel set around a lake and skating rink. One night, I received a surprise phone call from my parents who said, "We are going to be there tomorrow. We are coming after all!" I was so excited, I ran back to my room and jumped up and down on the bed. My roommate thought I was crazy because for the whole week I had been very quiet and pensive. I didn't sleep at all that night.

It was at those Junior Worlds that I met Gordeeva and Grinkov for the first time. I was totally impressed by their skating and never dreamt that someday I could be on the same podium. They were so good. After winning the Junior Worlds that year, they went on to win the Senior Worlds in 1985 and I don't know of anyone else who has done that. They were amazing skaters.

For the rest of the time I was in Colorado, I strived to make an effort to be around the other kids as much as possible and to learn English in the process. Because I was so introverted, I normally preferred to stay in but I had become friendly with some of the others, and on the last day of the competition, I decided to go to a party with the rest of the team. We were given a strict curfew of 11:30 p.m. but at 12:45 we were still partying. It wasn't in my nature to go against the rules but, for once, I was really having fun. Later, we snuck up the back stairs of the hotel and I led the way. At the top of the stairs, and just visible through the open door, was a pair of feet that belonged to the most feared representative of the Canadian Figure Skating Association (CFSA). Everyone hated it when this lady came to the rink during practices because she was so hard on the young skaters, making comments like, "I think you need to work on this, and if you don't get it, you can't compete." Even her appearance was intimidating to me; she had blond, teased hair and always wore big, round sun-glasses. It wasn't until many years later that we realized how good this woman had been for the team because she constantly pushed the kids to do better. But, back then, we were all afraid of her, especially me. When we reached the landing, there she was, with her hands on her hips, looking so stern, and lined up beside her were all the other team leaders. I was really afraid and kept my eyes down. Everyone got into a lot of trouble that night but this was one time when my not speaking English came in very handy because, when questioned, I just couldn't answer. In English or French, I was too scared and I was eventually let off with no discipline.

It wasn't until I started skating with Lloyd that I began to comprehend the English language. Before that, I could only greet people and speak the odd word. Most of the time, though, I would sit and pretend I was listening but I really didn't understand anything that was being said.

Lloyd

I thought Lorri and I would skate together forever, and when she told me she was quitting, I was devastated. I just couldn't understand. We were at Rink-in-the-Park in Kitchener, where we were training. I noticed Lorri had been talking with Mr. Leitch for a while, and as I came off the ice, we bumped into each other. She said, "Herbie, I have something to tell you."

I jokingly replied, "Oh yeah . . . you're quitting, right?" Lorri looked at me for a moment and then quietly said, "Yes, I am. I'm quitting."

I was floored . . . completely shocked and totally unaware she had even been contemplating this, and had no idea why. I didn't say a word but went back to the dressing room, took off my skates and threw them as hard as I could against the cement wall. The impact of the skates took a huge chunk out of the wall but I didn't care. I sat on the bench and cried for about an hour. We had skated together for eleven years and I figured, without Lorri, my career was finished. I didn't want to skate with anyone else, nor did I think anyone else would want to skate with me. In my eyes, it was all over.

After a while, Mr. Leitch came into the dressing room and we talked for a couple of hours. He said, "Don't worry, we will get you another partner. I think you should keep skating and it will all work out." But I wasn't ready to listen to him. I went home, told my parents, and from that April until the summer I missed a lot of skating sessions. My heart wasn't in it. Although deep down I hoped that Mr. Leitch would find me a new partner, I didn't do anything about it myself. I just hung around the rink and skated on my own.

I was also bitter with Lorri for a long time. We didn't speak for about two and a half years. When we were finally able to sit down and talk about it, I realized why she had quit. Her decision had nothing to do with us. She hadn't been able to cope with the discipline and training regimen at Mr. Leitch's school. Lorri had not been happy and wanted to move on with her life. Always more mature than I was, she was looking toward the future while I lived for the moment. When she explained things to me, it was suddenly clear why she had quit, but in the beginning it was very hard because my perception was distorted. I took her decision personally. Things were going so well for us and we had spent so much time together . . . skating . . . driving . . . going to all the competitions. All the hard work had been done with Lorri and everything that could have possibly happened, happened to Lorri and me.

I was glad when we were finally able to clear the air and Lorri and I are great friends today, but when she quit, I really thought my career was over. I mean, what options did I have? Although I had some success as a singles skater, I never considered for a moment taking it up again. I was a pairs skater first and foremost and I loved it. If I couldn't skate pairs, then I just wasn't going to skate at all.

A couple of months after Lorri and I split, Mark Rowson, a fellow skater who had also just broken up with his partner, arranged for a girl by the name of Kathy Matousek to try out with him. Mr. Leitch said that I should also try skating with her but I think, in retrospect, he just wanted me to feel better. So Kathy came out from Vancouver and skated with both Mark and me. After about a week, Mr. Leitch sat the three of us down and said he thought Kathy looked better with me. I was shocked because, although we did have big throws and could do all the things that were expected of us, I really thought that her trying out with me was more of an appease-ment on Mr. Leitch's part. Since Kathy had originally come to try out with Mark, Mr. Leitch gave her the choice of who she wanted to skate with. When she said, "I would like to skate with Lloyd," I couldn't believe it!

Kathy was so different from Lorri and in the beginning it was difficult to get used to each other. It wasn't that I compared her to my old partner. In fact, I was so angry with Lorri at the time that I put her completely out of my head. But since she and I had skated for so long together, we had formed a bond, in that we knew what the other was thinking all the time and how we would react in vari-ous situations out on the ice. Every time you start with a new part-ner, you have to learn all over again. It takes time and certainly doesn't happen overnight.

Kathy and I began skating together in July 1982 and, six weeks later, we competed internationally at the Coupe des Alpes competi-tion and came in second. It was a great way to start a new partner-ship. Kathy and I eventually grew to be good friends, but since she was younger than I was by two years, we led completely different lives when we were not skating. We never fought, though, and had an excellent rapport on the ice. I was older now and more mature. We were out there to get something accomplished,

I began university at McMaster in Hamilton in 1982, where I lived off-campus with some guys from school. On the first day, some students and I went to a bar between sessions and I sat down at a table with seven others. Five of us who met that day are still good friends.

For the first couple of years my schedule was really hectic because I commuted back and forth to train in Preston. I also had a part-time job at a convenience store. So my life at that time consisted of skating, working and school. I would get up at around 6:00 in the morning and drive to Preston, where I skated from 6:30 to 8:30, and then head back to Hamilton for class, which usually started at 9:30. If classes began at 8:30, I could skate for only an hour. I went to school until about 3:30 and then would head back to Preston to skate from 4:00 to 8:00 or 5:00 to 9:00, again depending on my classes. Once the skating was over, I returned to Hamilton to start work at 10:00 p.m. and usually managed to do some homework while I was at the store. My shift was over at 3:00 in the morning, and then I would catch a couple of hours of sleep and be up at 6:00 to start all over again. I had to work in the beginning because it was the only way I could afford to skate.

My friends from school, all non-skaters, treated me exactly as I wanted to be treated—like one of the guys. We were all in the physical education program and one friend in particular, Danny Walsh, was a real gem. He was instrumental in helping me get through university. Much the same as Pam had done for me in high school, Danny would pick up my work, find out when the exams were and assist me when I returned. He was a great person to have as a friend.

I was beginning to receive some recognition at this time because Lorri and I had been to Worlds the same year I started university. But it wasn't until I went to the Olympics two years later that I began to get more recognition at school. No one asked for autographs or anything like that but I heard comments such as, "Hey, there's the guy who went to the Olympics!"

Most of the professors were understanding about my schedule and treated me very well. But a few didn't like the fact that I was doing something other than academics. They wouldn't let me miss exams and would want to fail me because I was away for so many classes due to competing. This was even though I maintained an above 85 average. Those professors thought everything we did should be related to education and I had many run-ins with them. I often had to go to see the dean of the faculty. The professors would always lose out when I was forced to go over their heads and, as a result, their treatment of me was rather harsh at times. Overall, though, I found my university years to be wonderful and the work-load relatively easy. It took me six years to graduate but that was because I was there for only sixty percent of the time. What I really enjoyed was just being treated like a regular guy.

Isabelle

My parents and coaches started worrying about my small size when I was eleven because I had only reached the height of a nine year old. By the time I was twelve, they were really anxious as I was still only four foot seven. They wondered if I would ever grow to an average height and so I was taken to a hospital for tests. It wasn't unusual for someone in my family to be this small: Mom is only five feet tall and Dad and my brother are five foot seven. My tallest aunt was only four foot eleven. So everybody was very little . . . except that every-body else wasn't planning on a skating career.

The doctors determined that all of my energy was being used up in training, with nothing left over for growing. So they proposed hormones to slow down my puberty. They explained to my parents that, once I began menstruating, within two years I would stop growing and they were concerned that I wouldn't make it beyond four foot nine. The hormones would stop my puberty altogether and give me a longer time span to grow in. They expected by my taking them that I could reach between four foot eleven and five foot one.

I started the hormones when I was twelve years old. The pre-scription called for two pills, three times a day. They had to be taken in the morning, afternoon and at midnight. So, when I was asleep, I would have to be woken up to take the pills. My mom would give them to me and most of the time I didn't know what was going on because I would wake up in such a fog. She would put a glass of water to my mouth and hold her hand under my chin as she coaxed me to swallow the pills. More often than not, I would respond by telling her to leave me alone. During competitions or training, I had to remember to take them myself, so I would set my alarm clock.

The hormones were given to me under a doctor's prescription. Because they weren't steroids used to enhance performance, I didn't have any problems at competitions, although I did have to let officials know ahead of time, in writing, what I was taking.

As I continued with the hormone treatment, there didn't seem to be any side effects, but now my coaches and my dad began to worry that when I went off them I might mature too suddenly and gain a lot of weight. So, by the time I was sixteen, they began sending me to the gym to work out. I was put on a weight lifting and body building program for five days a week, two hours a session. The extra training produced the effect they wanted and I probably could have taken the hormones for another year, but when I was seventeen I grew tired of it all. I thought I was tall enough at five feet and I wanted only to experience what every other girl had experienced long before me. I went off the hormones and gained ten pounds, but with all the training at the gym I lost three percent of my fat. Any weight I had gained was muscle. I was so happy when I was able to stop because, at long last, I could finally grow up.

Lloyd

In 1983, Kathy and I competed at the Worlds in Helsinki, Finland, where we placed tenth, just behind Mark Rowson and his new partner, coincidentally. We were doing really well and to this day people say that Kathy and I performed the biggest throws they had ever seen.

Methods of training were changing somewhat as I grew older. The actual physical training became easier but the psychological side never changed. We have learned now that more is not necessarily better, but back then Mr. Leitch was still a real stickler about discipline and physical fitness. He would bring in experts to talk to us and then check our various levels of fitness and fat. We had to maintain both at a certain level or he would make us do more training. It was very difficult for many skaters.

Mr. Leitch always had other coaches with him as well as choreographers and ballet instructors. He had some teaching figures and others teaching singles but everyone was there to assist him. He was the head coach and was in complete control at all times. One of the coaches who taught pairs skating was Jamie McGrigor, who had skated with Mr. Leitch, then moved away to coach before returning to the school. I had known Jamie since I was nine years old and used to board at his parents' house in Preston while training for various competitions. At that time, he was already on the national and world teams and I really liked him. Jamie was a great guy and was instrumental in teaching Kathy and I to be good pairs skaters. Although Mr. Leitch was in charge and gave us a lot of attention and direction, it was Jamie who taught us the tricks of the trade. I would say he was the only person other than Mr. Leitch who helped Kathy and I achieve the success we did.

In 1984, we were on our way to Nationals. Our club had a betting pool going to see who would win the championship because Underhill and Martini had withdrawn due to an injury Barb had sustained. They were still going to the Worlds and Olympics but the three teams who could now vie for first place at Nationals were all training with Mr. Leitch. There were Kathy and me, Cynthia Coull and Mark Rowson and Melinda Kunhegyi and Lyndon Johnston. On any given day, any one of us could win. In 1983, Barb and Paul were national champions, Cynthia and Mark were second, Kathy and I were third and Melinda and Lyndon were fourth. All the way through the international competitions of that season, we flipflopped back and forth. But, in 1984, our club pool picked Cynthia and Mark or Melinda and Lyndon to win. The only person who chose Kathy and me was Jamie. Because Barb and Paul obviously had a buy to Worlds and the Olympics, only two of our teams would be allowed to both competitions if we placed first, second and third. Our coaches asked us to consider allowing the team that placed first to go to both the Olympics and Worlds, and the teams that placed second and third to split between the two competitions, so all three of our teams would be able to compete in at least one of the two events. Jamie took Kathy and me aside and convinced us not to consider it because, he said, "You guys are going to win anyway and are going to go to both places. Don't even think for a moment you won't go anywhere." So we listened to Jamie and didn't opt for our coaches' plan. We said that we would rather go along with whoever came first and second going to both places and leaving it at that.

As it turned out, Kathy and I skated phenomenally and we won our first national championship. I even think we were good enough to beat Underhill and Martini but I really don't know if the politics of skating would have allowed us to win if they had competed. I do know that, once the Olympics came, Barb and Paul skated abysmally, placing seventh, and Kathy and I again skated great. In fact, we couldn't have skated any better and yet we placed eighth. Two weeks later, Barb and Paul skated outstandingly at the Worlds and won the championship. Kathy and I skated well again and moved up to fifth in the world in only two weeks. The higher Underhill and Martini rose, the better we did. Politics, of course, has a lot to do with that.

Isabelle

I never had an idol in figure skating but in Barbara Underhill and Paul Martini I did have role models. There was one incident involving them that I remember clearly and often helped me throughout my future career.

I had watched the 1984 Olympics on television, when Barb and Paul fell during their competition. Two weeks later, the Worlds were held in Ottawa and my parents surprised Pascal and I by announcing they were going to take us to see it. We didn't have any tickets but we took a chance and drove to the capital city, where we were only able to get seats way up in the "nosebleed" section. But I didn't care; I was just so excited to be there.

Barb and Paul won the championship and I couldn't believe that they could have fallen only two weeks before and then come back to win the gold. It was such an inspiration to me. Later on in my career, when I would fall or miss a jump, I would think, That's okay because it is possible to get back up and go on to do well. There is sunshine out there somewhere if you keep working toward your goal.

I also remember seeing Lloyd and Kathy compete at those same Worlds and admiring how they started their program with a huge throw triple loop but that is all I remember . . . that and the fact they wore black and red costumes for their short program. Apparently they skated very well but all I recall now is the opening throw and the color of their outfits—sorry, Lloyd!

When Pascal and I won the junior competition at Nationals in 1985, it felt really good. We skated well and were on our way to the 1986 Junior Worlds in Yugoslavia, where I was to meet my now good friend Kristi Yamaguchi for the first time.

The year before, Kristi had been skating in singles as well as pairs but wasn't at the Junior Worlds in 1985. Her partner, Rudy Galindo, who was very tiny, competed in the singles event and I remember people saying that this little guy had a partner back home who could perform really difficult jumps. I remember thinking that no little girl could do the jumps they were talking about and really didn't believe them. Well, Kristi attended Junior Worlds in 1986, and she was as little as I was, if not smaller. She competed in pairs and singles and it was true—she could do all the jumps, no matter how difficult. I was impressed.

Kurt Browning was also around during my early competitive years. We became quite close and after a while began noticing that the same things seemed to happen to both of us at the same time. For example, when I placed fifth at junior and then won junior, Kurt did exactly the same thing. We had the same standings at the competitions and followed each other all the time. Kurt and I went on to become really good friends and, throughout our relationship, more coincidences have happened than either of us can ever explain. A few years ago I had a car accident, and two weeks later so did he. I was once dating someone seriously at the same time Kurt was and both couples broke up within the same three weeks. When I purchased my first home, he bought his that same week. But when

Kurt announced his engagement in April 1995, I looked at him and said, "This is it now . . . I am going a different way than you." He replied, "Okay, since this is a pretty big move, I will give you a two-year raincheck." I was relieved because at the time I had no intention of marrying anyone. As it happened, I too became engaged, to U.S. pairs skater Rocky Marvel, only six months later.

On the way home from the Junior Worlds, I had quite an experience. The weather was very bad and late one night we had to take a bus to catch a train that was leaving at midnight. We arrived at the station, left our luggage on the platform and then prepared to get on the train. It was an old-fashioned type where the luggage had to be passed through the windows. As we began to board, someone yelled to us that it was the wrong car and that ours was down at the other end. So we ran to the proper car and again, as we started to climb in, someone else informed us that we had been right the first time and we had to go back. Now, it was really getting late and Josée, Pascal and almost everybody else were finally aboard, except for me and the team leader and another skater. One of them was passing the luggage through the windows and the other was holding the tickets for the entire team. All of a sudden, the train started pulling away so we began to yell, "Stop! Stop the train!" On the platform, there were some soldiers who were also supposed to be on the train and they began to shout too. Finally the train stopped and we jumped in. I tried to sleep but the poor soldiers got drunk and were crying and carrying on because they were leaving for war and so it was impossible to get any rest. It turned out that the one fellow who threw the luggage on board left his own bags back at the station. It was a lot to go through for a fourteen year old who hated being away from home and couldn't speak any English.

Lloyd

My first Olympics was an amazing experience and was everything I expected it to be. I was rooming with one of my best friends, John Thomas, who was a dancer, and thoroughly enjoyed sharing it all with him. We were there for the pure enjoyment and everything knocked us out, from getting our uniforms, to walking into the opening ceremonies with the rest of the Canadian team.

Since there was no snow in Sarajevo when we arrived, the officials had to cancel the ski events. Then it began to snow and didn't stop for four days. Ski competitions that had reopened were now closed again because it was snowing too much! The people were very friendly and would take us wherever we wanted to go, and although the downtown area was beautiful, I do recall seeing people walking around with guns.

When our competitions were over, John and I really took advantage of being away in this glorious setting. We would put on our Sarajevo sweaters that we had made for us while we were there, pack a couple of small tote bags with beer and walk through the streets, having a wonderful time mixing with the people.

We made it to the ladies' event because, of course, we couldn't miss seeing our Canadians, and although we were a little under the weather, so to speak, we were there to cheer them on. When the Canadian hockey team was playing Czechoslovakia and had a chance to win a medal, we wanted to be in attendance at this important event as well. We decided to go to the game with the bobsled team who was staying in the same housing with us. All of us had become very friendly during the course of the Games. They had a big truck that was used to transport the sleds and offered to drive us. The truck, which still had a sled in it, was loaded with beer and about fifteen or twenty guys and gals, and we spent the next three hours just driving around the town. At one point, John had to go to the bathroom urgently. We stopped at a light, lifted up the back door of the truck and John relieved himself right there, amid all of the traffic.

Eventually, we found our way to the game where poor John was thrown out for being a little too vocal. His accreditation was taken away and our officials had to get involved in order to reinstate him. But it was all so much fun and it is hard to hear about what is going on now. John and I often speak about Sarajevo and it is difficult for us to think about the times we had that were so memorable. I think of walking down those streets then . . . now, there is nothing there.

Isabelle

Although I was skating an awful lot as a teenager, I never felt as if I was missing out on anything because I really didn't like parties or socializing all that much anyway. I was always so tired when I arrived home from training that I only wanted to relax and read a book or just sit and have some quiet time to myself. I also never felt comfortable at parties, partly because I was so tiny and shy. I didn't begin to date until I was seventeen, although I did go to my prom. I was sixteen, and because I didn't have a boyfriend, I went with a fellow skater and good friend, Jean-Michel Bombardier. We had known each other since we were eleven and trained together every day. I guess my life as a teenager pretty well revolved around skating.

My coaches and training remained the same during those years and continued to do so until Lloyd and I began skating together. Josée and Eric taught Pascal and I everything, including how to do the lifts and throws we used.

I was never afraid of the lifts but I wasn't too crazy about throws. Even certain jumps would make me nervous. Sometimes, as I was learning a particular one, I would skate around and do all the preparation for it but at the last minute I wouldn't jump. I was afraid of it. I would turn around and try again but then I would falter and my coaches would become angry. The throws are scary too, but if I was afraid, and I often was in the beginning, I would somehow manage to stop.

My father was still really involved in my career. Mom was, too, but not in the same way. She loved coming to competitions and she and Josée would look after my costumes and how I looked. Dad, on the other hand, was more technical. While my mom would sit and enjoy my competitions, Dad couldn't watch because he got so nervous. He would come to the competition and watch everyone else, but as soon as it was my turn, he would go out and have a cup of coffee. While he made me nervous during practices, his being at my competitions never bothered me and, in fact, I actually preferred it if both my parents were there.

If I didn't do well at a competition, my dad would get very angry with me and sometimes threaten to pull me out of skating, but my mom never got upset. She would always give me a big hug no matter how I did.

Lloyd

Even though I was older and supposedly wiser, I still got into trouble with Mr. Leitch because I was always trying to break the rules. I missed sessions and would receive lengthier lectures than I did when I was a kid, about taking on more responsibilities and how my behavior was not befitting a person of my age.

Once, a few of us got into trouble and had to run fifteen miles as our punishment. Mr. Leitch stood there and watched. But that was nothing compared to the twenty-five miles we had to run as discipline following another one of our escapades. Some of us had been partying the night before and one of the group missed the morning session. Mr. Leitch had also received calls from people who had seen us out and thought we had been drinking. So we got a heavy lecture and had to run twenty-five miles. I ran the whole distance because I am the type of person who won't let anybody win over me. I made the punishment into a little competition. In my mind, if I had refused, Mr. Leitch would have won . . . so I ran and I would think, Hey, no matter what you throw at me, I can give it back. It wasn't spite or anything like that; it was more to prove that I could do it. That attitude is probably the reason why I survived so long in the skating world and am still skating today.

At the level I was then at, it cost my parents about $25,000 a year for me to skate, but I finally started to get a little more funding from the government and from the CFSA which added up to about $5,000 a year. As well, Kathy and I were doing well enough by then to be invited to exhibitions and carnivals, and those types of events also helped to pay the bills. Because we were amateurs and weren't allowed to take money, we had to arrange to have any payment deposited into a trust fund; we could then submit receipts and obtain some of it back.

Kathy and I didn't get a chance to compete at the 1985 Nationals because she was injured and we had to withdraw. Although my partner wasn't one hundred percent by the time the Worlds were scheduled, she was a little better and we decided to skate. I remember thinking, Oh my God, this is just like Barb and Paul's situation the year before.

Everything went smoothly in practice. We were skating well and just hoped that we could keep it together for another week. The competition for the short program finally arrived and we skated fantastically, ending up third. We probably should have won that program because the two teams that performed before us missed their jumps, but we were happy because we had skated so well. In the long program, we did well enough to come third and receive a bronze medal. I was ecstatic.

After the competition, we went on the International Skating Union (ISU) World Tour in Japan for the next three and a half weeks and it was terrific. Katarina Witt and Brian Orser were also there and I have to say that it was one of the best tours I have ever done through Asia.

Kathy decided to quit skating after that, partly because she had shin splints and stress fractures in both legs. The constant pounding was hurting her. We had huge throws and, back then, the bigger the throws were, the better the judges liked it, and I think it was too much for her physically. She also missed her home in Vancouver. She was 5,000 miles away from her family and I think it put quite a burden on her. Kathy was ready to quit and move on to something else. I had found out how she felt earlier in the year, when she admitted that she was unsure about continuing

I was fine with her decision. I had been through it before and I wasn't angry, but I did wonder what was wrong. I thought that maybe it was something I was doing, or perhaps something Mr.

Leitch was doing, that made these girls want to leave skating. I just wasn't sure.

After Kathy left, I wondered if I wanted another partner, and although Mr. Leitch assured me I would find someone else and had several girls try out with me, I knew it would be difficult to find the right person. I had heard of a girl in Toronto by the name of Karen Westby who was a great singles skater and who wanted to try pairs. Without Mr. Leitch, I went to Toronto and tried out with her, although I was uneasy about working with someone who had never skated pairs. But it wasn't too bad. It was definitely not as easy as it had been with Kathy and Lorri but it also wasn't overly difficult. So I went back to Preston and discussed the matter with Mr. Leitch, who did not think it was a great idea. But it was already getting close to summer and I thought if I didn't skate with Karen, I would wind up missing the whole year. So against Mr. Leitch's better judgment, I agreed to skate with her.

Karen and I didn't compete internationally at all. We made it to the 1986 Nationals in North Bay and skated well but we came in third, and for the first time in six years I didn't make the world team, since only two couples were allowed to go that year. It was at that point that I started becoming vocal about the judging and I believed I had good reason to. We came second in the short program but we should have won. There was no doubt about it. The judges dumped us and I believed that they did it because of me—because Karen was my third partner and I thought they were thinking, Why doesn't he get out of the sport?

Being on the world team is very special and when I didn't make it, I was really hurt. I remember Mr. Leitch coming into the dressing room as I was walking out. He gave me a big bear hug and I stood and cried in his arms for fifteen minutes. My coach tried to calm me by saying that things would get better but I didn't believe him. I was too upset.

Later on, I said some things at a press conference, where I blasted the association, its president and the judging and accused them of showing favoritism. I was really harsh on everybody. The things I said appeared in a big article in the newspapers a few days later and the association called Mr. Leitch and asked him what I was doing and why I was saying all these things. They were furious with me but I didn't care because I strongly believed Karen and I had been rooked. When I heard their reaction, I thought, I don't want anything more to do with these people. I was fed up and so I quit. I also believed that was what they wanted anyway . . . to get rid of me. So I called an end to my skating career two weeks after the 1986 Nationals.

My parents had moved from Seaforth to Kitchener in 1984 because my dad was working in the area. I went home and took on two jobs at different bars and for a year I didn't skate and made absolutely no plans. I worked a lot and partied a lot and soon lost track of the skaters in the area. Although I made new friends at the bars, I was really just hanging out and doing nothing.

Isabelle

At the 1986 Nationals, Pascal and I were competing at the senior level where we placed fifth, but my partner had been showing signs of discontent for a while. He just didn't like the sport anymore and thought there was too much pressure. That year, Pascal caught mononucleosis and was out for some time. When he got better, he was about to come back when he had an accident on a motorbike and broke his elbow. In September, a few weeks later, he returned with a cast. We were scheduled for a competition and so we were training hard because he had been away so long. He skated for one week and then said, "I don't want to do this anymore," and he quit.

I was saddened to hear of his decision because I had had high hopes that we would go far together. It was difficult for me but I also felt that if he didn't want to do it anymore there was nothing I could do.

I was only sixteen years old and I wanted to skate with another partner. I didn't feel as if my career was finished but it would be hard to find someone who was at my level. There just weren't too many guys out there who knew how to skate pairs.

While my coaches were looking for someone else, I decided, since I had been skating some singles, to try it just for fun. I won at the provincials and the top two skaters at that competition had the choice of skating at either Nationals or the Canada Games. I decided on the Canada Games because there was no pairs competition there. Nationals were being held three weeks before the Games, and if you wanted to be in them you had to go through Divisionals first and place in the top eight. The Divisionals came and went but I didn't have to bother with them.

Three weeks before Nationals, I received a phone call and was informed I couldn't compete at the Canada Games because I was a carded athlete, that is, I received money from the government because I was in the top group at Senior Nationals and I was top junior. I was upset and said, "But that was in pairs; this is singles." Although we fought it, I wasn't allowed to compete at the Games and so they had to give me a buy at Nationals because the whole thing wasn't my fault. So, that year, instead of sixteen ladies there were seventeen; that had never happened before and hasn't happened since, as far as I know. I ended up finishing sixth in novice, which was pretty good for someone who had never competed in singles at that level.

Lloyd

In December 1986, the Junior World Championships were being held in Kitchener and, because I lived in the area, I was asked to be one of the assistant team leaders for the junior world team. I thought, Well, it's going to be in Kitchener and since I know most of the kids, why not? So I went as a CFSA official.

At the competition, I saw a good friend of mine named Bob Young. Bob was from the United States and I had known him since I was eleven years old. We talked a lot and he believed from the way I was speaking that I wasn't ready to quit skating. Quite frankly, I didn't know what I wanted to do. I also met and spoke with Josée Picard and Eric Gillies, who had a team competing at the event.

After we talked for a while, they asked, "Why don't you come and try out with Isabelle Brasseur?" I thought, Isabelle Brasseur . . . she is a tiny little kid and is not a strong skater. It would never work . . . I mean, why?

The first time I saw Isabelle skate was in 1982, when we were competing in a fours competition at Nationals in Brandon, Manitoba. There was a little wee team of four, somewhere between the ages of nine and eleven years old, and one of those pairs was Isabelle and Pascal. I thought they were cute little kids but never believed they would go anywhere because the boy was too small. I also thought Isabelle was weak and that she would never grow. I think everyone's basic impression of Isabelle at a young age was, Oh, look how tiny she is. She seemed so frail, as if you could just touch her and she would break. The next time I recall seeing them was in 1983 at Nationals in Montreal. I think Isabelle and Pascal were probably novice at that time and to me she sort of looked like Shirley Temple, with the big, puffy hair and all the curls and braces. But, from then on, we were aware of who they were because they were actually doing quite well. The first time we competed against them was in 1986, when I think they placed fifth to Karen's and my third. But it never crossed my mind when I watched her and Pascal that I would ever be asked to skate with her someday. Not in a million years.

Although I hadn't missed skating in the slightest, I started to think about what Bob had said. I also mulled over Josée and Eric's request and thought, Oh, what the heck. I have nothing else to do; I'll go. I was overweight and out of shape and figured I had nothing to lose.

Isabelle

In December 1986, just before I competed at Nationals as a single, a pair of my fellow skaters, Jean-Michel Bombardier and Marie-Josée Fortin (Mimi), had made it to Junior Worlds in Kitchener. Of course, Josée and Eric went with them and, while there, they met up with Lloyd. According to Josée, when they found out Lloyd wasn't skating, my coaches informed him that I had stopped skating pairs as well and that they were looking for a new partner. They suggested he try out with me. I guess Lloyd wasn't too sure because he was concerned about my size. But apparently Josée and Eric told him that I had grown quite a bit in the past six months and developed into a better skater. And it was true; I had become much stronger since they put me in the special training program. I then received a phone call from Josée, who asked, "Do you want to try out with Lloyd?" I started to cry and told her I didn't want to because he was so big and I really believed I could wind up seriously injured and in a wheelchair within a year if I skated with him.

Although I didn't know Lloyd personally, I had seen him skate, the last time being at the 1986 Nationals. When we were younger, I also recall seeing him sitting in the stands at some of our competitions. He looked so big to me, and before we skated he used to say to Pascal, *"Va pisser dans le vent,"* which loosely translates as, "Go pee in the wind." I have no idea what he meant, and when I eventually mentioned it to Lloyd after we began skating together, he couldn't recollect ever having said that. But I remember it.

When I hung up from Josée, I was absolutely positive I didn't want to skate with Lloyd and it took her about two weeks to convince me otherwise. They had already invited him down and had to go back and say to him, "Well, we think we may have to wait a little bit. There is a small problem but we will try to fix it." In my mind, this was no small problem! I was afraid of Lloyd because of his age and size. I had also heard rumors his partners may have been injured from their huge throws. I was definitely afraid and it took a lot of talking on my coaches' part to persuade me to meet with Lloyd. But if someone had asked me earlier if I ever thought I would skate with him, my answer would have been a resounding "No!" I never thought I would or could. I was just too scared.

CHAPTER THREE

A New Beginning

Isabelle

AFTER SPEAKING to Josée, I immediately went to my father and begged him not to force me to skate with Lloyd. "He is too big and I'm afraid!" I cried. But both my parents and coaches urged me to try just once. They reminded me that it was a rare opportunity to be able to skate with a world medalist and that I may never have the chance again.

The coaxing continued for another two weeks as I steadfastly resisted their arguments. Finally, Josée and Eric said to me, "Try it for us. You have been skating for so long and we would just like to see what happens. We promise you won't have to skate with him after the tryout if you don't want to." They and my parents also promised not to leave me alone with him. I was so shy and nervous. In fact, my dad agreed that he and my mother would take time off work to be there with me during the tryout.

I could see how important it was to everyone and so, to make them happy, I reluctantly agreed to skate with Lloyd. My family and coaches would be with me, so what could happen? I will try out and that will be it, I thought. And I won't have to hear about it anymore.

Lloyd wasn't scheduled to come for a few days yet, and although I tried to put the whole thing out of my mind, I was still extremely anxious. Never once did I really think anything would come of it—nor did I want anything to.

The day of the tryout finally arrived, and in spite of my nerves I couldn't help feeling a little excited. No matter how much I stated that I didn't want to skate with Lloyd, part of me was actually looking forward to it. I had been training on my own for a few months and missed skating pairs.

I was out on the ice when Lloyd stepped into the arena. I stared at him for a moment and then skated over to a friend of mine. "Oh my God. Look at him!" I said. "I can't believe we are going to skate together. He is so big. How am I ever going to follow him?" I never thought it would work. Never. He appeared to be so strong while I felt very small in comparison and I wondered how on earth I would ever keep up with him.

Lloyd

I don't think I had any expectations regarding the outcome of the two-day tryout. If anything, I was experiencing doubt during my drive to Montreal. I had mixed feelings about everything and was even wondering if I wanted to come out of retirement.

It was December 21 and my 1982 diesel Chevette was handling the journey just fine. Before I left, I remember my father saying, "The Chevette will make it. Just don't drive it too hard." My dad was so easygoing and positive about everything.

Mom, on the other hand, was worrying about the wisdom of me taking the trip in the first place. She said, "I don't know if you should go. Maybe you should just call them and say, 'I've thought about it. I've had my place in the sun and it's time to move on.'" But something told me I had to make this trip. I had to try this.

I think my best friends, Pam and John Boniferro, played a big part in my decision to go. Pam and John are married now but at that time John was the manager at one of the bars where I worked and

Pam was his girlfriend. We had become very close during that year, and when I asked them what they thought, they told me that if I didn't go, I would probably wonder about it for the rest of my life. They didn't care about my skating as much as they cared about me and they knew that I would regret it if I didn't go.

Despite their encouragement, I still found myself wondering during that long drive if I was doing the right thing and why I was even bothering. I knew who Isabelle was and I was really skeptical about the whole situation. I didn't think it was going to work. But I believed then, as I do now, that if you don't try you will never know the outcome, good or bad. I also rationalized that this experience might be a last attempt for me to say farewell to skating. I thought it was probably a waste of time, but by at least trying, I would have given it a shot and maybe then I could finally say, It's time to do something else with my life.

When I reached Boucherville, I drove straight to the rink, following the instructions I had received from Josée. It was a regular-looking complex, with nothing special about it; two rinks, side by side, with a little cafeteria upstairs. I walked in, with my favorite skate bag slung over my shoulder. I had received it at my first international competition, in 1978, and as a matter of fact I still use it today. I spotted Josée and Eric, and when I walked over to speak to them, I realized that Isabelle's whole family was at the rink to view the tryout.

Isabelle was on the ice and when I first saw her I was really surprised. I thought, Wow, she has grown. Her face had matured since I last saw her the year before. Yet she was still very tiny and didn't appear to have gained any weight. Her coaches and her dad were bilingual, so with their assistance we introduced ourselves and talked for a while. But Isabelle and I were unable to communicate directly. It was very informal and didn't bother me a bit. What concerned me was the fact that I was out of shape and hadn't worn those skates for six months. I didn't even know how sharp they were.

I went to the dressing room and put on the only outfit I had brought. It was an ugly, blue thing, with a big red stripe down the side, that I had used for practice years ago. Now, after living the "good life" for the last few months, it was the only one that fit. As I stepped out onto the ice, I was a little bit uneasy. Usually, I find that, even after not skating for a while, I can come back without too much trouble, but this time I felt out of shape and it didn't help that all these people were watching me. With the impression that I must have been making on Isabelle and her family, thank goodness my expectations of the tryout weren't all that high anyway.

Isabelle

Josée and Eric introduced Lloyd and me and we greeted each other in our own languages. But even though we couldn't understand each other, we got along well right from the start.

Lloyd immediately showed his gentle side, which made me feel at ease. I think he knew I was scared and he smiled at me. His eyes seemed to say, "Don't worry. I won't hurt you." After that, he was so nice to me out on the ice, and if one of the other skaters came in my direction, he would pick me up to ensure my safety. Because of his thoughtfulness, I relaxed very quickly.

I knew Lloyd was good. I had seen him skate before and realized what he was capable of, and when he got on the ice, he was exactly as I expected. You would never have known that he hadn't been on skates for six months and I was worried, thinking, How are we ever going to match?

We began to skate, and before I knew it, the session was over and I had loved it. I thought it was absolutely amazing because I could keep up and do all these things. I went home that day so excited and couldn't wait to go back. I remember the first twist we did: it made my heart feel ticklish, as if I were on a rollercoaster. It was exhilarating!

At the start of the session, Josée and Eric made me feel as if I was in control, asking me if I was okay with whatever it was they wanted performed. They were very calm and I eventually tried every element. I could even do the throws, which I hadn't thought I could do. I didn't believe I could land one with Lloyd, but on the second day we were landing a triple Salchow. I was just blown away by it all. I thought, If we can do that in a couple of days, imagine what we can accomplish in a few years!

When the tryout was over, I stepped off the ice and walked up to Josée, Eric and my parents and said, "Well, I skated with him, as you had asked, and I've made up my mind. I don't want to skate with anyone else!"

We had decided to go to a nice restaurant so we could all become better acquainted. We were also hoping to find out what Lloyd was thinking about the tryout. My coaches and my parents asked me to drive with him to the restaurant in case he couldn't find his way. Suddenly we were alone for the first time. Although I was still a little shy and there wasn't much conversation, I wasn't at all uncomfortable. In fact, I had a really good feeling about the two of us.

Lloyd

I stepped out onto the ice and Josée called Isabelle and me over. We chatted in a triangular fashion. Isabelle spoke French to her coach, who translated into English. I then spoke English to Josée and she repeated what I said to Isabelle in French. Once our instructions for the session were understood, we began with some stroking and singles skating.

It was awkward for me because I felt off balance and out of shape. Here I was—a guy who had been to the Olympics, was Canadian champion and third in the world—and I was skating as if I didn't deserve to be novice champion.

We hardly did any pairs elements in the first hour and during that time mainly performed side-by-side spins and jumps. I believe the reason for this was that Josée and Eric, who were running the session, were still trying to convince Isabelle that I should be there. I'm not sure that Isabelle even wanted to be at that tryout.

The session lasted for about three hours and, when it was completed, we had run through everything except the throws. We had done all the lifts and twists and even performed a split triple twist. Isabelle and I had done everything that I had performed with my old partner but we had done it all within the first three hours!

After we finished skating that first day, Isabelle went home and I followed Josée and Eric to their place, which was an hour and fifteen minutes from the rink. I intentionally avoided making any judgments during that drive, preferring to take a more laid-back attitude . . . Yes, we can do it. She's pretty small and I'm fairly big but the elements . . . we can do them. Once back at Josée and Eric's house, we sat and talked. Josée asked me what I thought. She and Eric were obviously promoting Isabelle to me but I still didn't want to commit and all I said was, "Well, it was pretty good and I can't believe we did it all."

The next day, we skated again and it was even better than the day before. We tried the throws and landed them all. Some were landed on one foot but most were on two, which I had expected because Isabelle was so small. It was then that I realized how good the pairs elements were. I began comparing us to the teams that we would have to compete against in a year's time. Could we do it?

After dinner at L'Artisan with Isabelle, her family and her coaches, I went back to Josée and Eric's, where we talked more seriously. They had videotaped the sessions and told me they thought it looked good. But I was unable to give them an answer then and there. I knew Isabelle and I could do the skating. We could handle everything, but I had a lot of unanswered questions that were much more difficult to deal with than the skating and I needed some time to sort them out.

What worried me most was Mr. Leitch's reaction; he had been against even my trying out with Isabelle. I wondered if he could be part of the coaching team since it had been made clear to me that Isabelle did not want to leave her coaches and her family. That would mean I would have to move to Montreal, unless we could train in both places.

I didn't decide anything at that time. I was heading back home for Christmas and Josée and Eric said they wanted to talk things over with Isabelle and her family. They told me they would call during the holidays. Now it was only a matter of logistics. Skating together had been no problem. Yet if Isabelle and I agreed to team up, I wondered how it was going to work and whether I would have the support of the man I owed my career to—Mr. Leitch.

Isabelle

I couldn't wait until we received Lloyd's answer, and until I heard I just kept hoping. Skating with him meant everything to me now but I knew he had a lot to face when he got home.

My moving to Ontario and training with Lloyd's coach was out of the question. I was too young and unsure of myself. And because I didn't speak English, I didn't know how I would be able to go to school. If necessary, I would have gone to Preston for the summer and had him come to Montreal for the winter. But I really preferred to stay with my coaches. Our tryout together had been the greatest thing to me and I only hoped that Lloyd was feeling the same way and would somehow be able to work it out.

Lloyd

The first place I stopped when I arrived home was Pam and John's. I had brought back the videotape of my tryout with Isabelle and asked them to take a look at it. Now, my friends knew absolutely nothing about figure skating but I watched their faces as they viewed the tape. The more I saw their expressions, the more I believed that I had been right: the pairs elements were good and if there was ever a partner that I could skate well with, it was Isabelle.

I next went to my parents, who plied me with a million and one questions. My dad asked, "Well, how did it feel?" I said, "It was good." We discussed the logistics of moving and he wondered if I would be able to get a job in Montreal and whether I would have a difficult time with the language. He then paused for a moment before quietly asking, "Do you really think it will work?" I told him that I thought it would but also expressed my concern that we would need to improve in some areas, especially the throws.

This bothered me a little because Kathy and I had been known for our throws: they had been the biggest in the world. I realized that Isabelle and I wouldn't have those same throws but I also knew beyond a doubt that everything else would be better. We would have to work on the throws. Although they would probably never be our strong point, I wondered if they could be good enough to get us through because I believed that, with everything else we had together, we would be better than our competitors. My dad told me that, whatever I decided, he would be behind me.

My mother had an entirely different opinion. In general, she tends to be more of a negative person but usually supports me in whatever I do. Yet, this time, my mom was definitely not enthusiastic. She believed I should quit skating, thinking I was too old. I guess she thought it was time I went out and made some money, perhaps by coaching. If I had stayed with Mr. Leitch, I probably could have done as she suggested but it was not in my plans. I never wanted to coach. She was also concerned about Isabelle's size and age and thought that I should let Isabelle have the chance to team up with another partner.

By the time I went to meet with Mr. Leitch, I think, subconsciously, I had already made up my mind. I just hadn't admitted it at that point, nor had I made any decisions about the coaching or how it was going to work. I thought by talking to Mr. Leitch, somehow, everything would fall together. It didn't—it fell apart.

Mr. Leitch viewed the tape, and although he had good things to say, he was critical as well. He also insisted that, if I decided to skate with Isabelle, he would be the head coach, meaning he would travel to our competitions with us. But he definitely wasn't excited about me skating with her. I think he felt that way because he had not initiated the meeting between her and me and because he didn't come to Montreal with me.

Mr. Leitch is the type of person who needs to be in control. I recognize this trait because I am the same way. The meeting didn't end on a positive note. I told him that I would have to discuss the matter more fully with Josée and Eric.

Isabelle's coaches were emphatic when I spoke with them. "We want to be the head coaches and we want you to train here. Isabelle will not go to Ontario because she is too young and doesn't speak the language. She also feels very comfortable with Josée."

So everything came down to me making the most difficult decision of my life. If I decided to go to Montreal, I would be leaving Mr. Leitch for good. There was no alternative because that's the way the coaching world is: "It is either my way or the highway." They tell the skater how it is going to be, and if the skater doesn't like it, he or she is free to go somewhere else. But if I stayed with him, I wouldn't be skating at all. My career would be finished. He didn't have anyone in mind who I could team up with. We were already halfway through the season and competitions had begun. People were training for Nationals and there were no other partners.

To leave Mr. Leitch was almost unthinkable. I had been with him for fifteen years and he was instrumental in everything I had done, from my early tests to my becoming national champion and placing third in the world. Without the discipline that Mr. Leitch taught me, I don't think I would have made it. I may have had the talent to succeed but I had many outside interests and diversions that may have stopped me had he not stepped in. Yes, there was no question that I owed my whole career to him and I didn't feel good about what was happening, but ultimately I had to make the decision.

I sat down with my parents again and told them what had transpired with Mr. Leitch. Dad said, "If you think the move is something you want and you believe in it, then go for it."

My mother offered me an opposite viewpoint. "I don't think it will work. You will be wasting your time, and I believe you are going to get down there and three months later you will be back home. By then you will have burned your bridges with Mr. Leitch."

Confused and disheartened, I went to Pam and John and asked for their opinions. They proceeded to ask me questions that had not come up with Mr. Leitch, Josée, Eric or my parents. Pam and John asked, "Are you old enough to make it work? Have you learned enough from Mr. Leitch? Can you take what you have learned here and use it somewhere else?"

They also wondered if I really needed a coach anymore. On reflection, I realized that I probably didn't because there wasn't much that I couldn't do technically. What I needed now was someone to contribute creative ideas and manage my career, pushing it perhaps in a different direction.

Pam and John put the situation in perspective for me. Everyone else had been too involved and unable to tap into what I required at this stage in my career. What I had to do was suddenly crystal clear.

I arranged another meeting with Mr. Leitch and came right out and told him I was going. He looked at me in amazement and said, "I can't believe that you are being so disloyal and that you would leave me after fifteen years. I have taught you for so long and always been there for you."

It was true. He had pulled me out of some tough situations where my mouth had gotten me into trouble with the association and other people. Yet I didn't believe that I was being disloyal to him. I just felt as if I was making a change. I saw the situation as an opportunity that was taking me to a different place and I had hoped for his blessing. To be quite honest, if I had been realistic, I would have seen this coming. The skating world is very cutthroat and few coaches are good friends with their students because many skaters leave on bad terms. Once I had heard Mr. Leitch's reaction, I knew beyond a doubt that I was leaving for good. There was no coming back.

I informed everyone of my decision and my news was received with mixed emotions. Josée and Eric were very happy. My dad simply accepted it and told me he would help me pack the car when the time came, whereas my mother informed me that she thought I wasn't making the right choice.

Once my mind had been made up, we didn't discuss it anymore and I spent a wonderful Christmas with my family. I also saw Pam and John often over the next couple of weeks. I liked being with them because they understood. I knew I could go over there and we would talk about everything but my impending move. So on January 7, 1987, Dad and I loaded up my Chevette and, at the age of twenty-three, I set out for a new beginning.

Isabelle

I was overjoyed when I heard the news. Lloyd had made the decision to skate with me and I knew how difficult this must have been for him. If it had been me who had to leave my coaches, I would have had a really hard time doing that. So I was grateful Lloyd understood that I had a problem with moving and that it probably wouldn't have worked if I had gone there.

Since I was a child, I never thought I was talented enough to make it anywhere but I always dreamt. I wanted to be on the top one day and that kept me working. Even if I really didn't think I could make it, I continually told myself, That is what you want. Go back to the rink and work hard and do what they tell you to do and someday, just maybe, you will make it. When I skated with Lloyd those two days, I could see the potential for us. We could do everything, and so when I heard that he was going to be my partner, those dreams now seemed possible. They were alive again.

I had been concerned about our age difference; I was only sixteen, and with Lloyd being seven years older, Josée and Eric wanted to make sure that he wouldn't quit after a year or so. But he promised that he would skate for at least another four years unless, of course, we didn't get along.

Lloyd

I finally arrived in Montreal and settled in at Josée and Eric's, where I was to stay for the next seven months. They had a chalet located in the woods on the back side of a ski hill in a little town called Bromont. It was a gorgeous place and my idea of perfect living.

First, though, I had to get a job. I noticed when I first arrived at the training center that there was no off-ice program. Nothing. I had come from a school where off-ice training was as important as on-ice training, and which had the facilities for this. But this center was very different. There were no amenities; no weight or ballet rooms, no warm-up area and only a very poor sound system.

At the time I left Preston, we had these extras in place *and* ice time at other arenas as well. On a scale of one to ten, the center in Boucherville was a one. I mean, it was awful. It was not a training center, as far as I was concerned. It was more like a rink where only a few people skated.

I had my aerobic instructor's license, and because I saw that the kids weren't getting off-ice training at the center, I approached Josée and Eric and asked them if I could teach aerobics to the kids. I figured I could get them in shape and skating well and the money would obviously help me out. Josée and Eric thought it was a fantastic idea and agreed immediately. So, in a wee closet of a room, I began teaching aerobics to their students.

Isabelle

Lloyd was no sooner down when he began giving aerobics classes to us. I had no choice; I had to take them along with the other students. Was he tough! His classes were so difficult that we could not walk the next day.

At the time, I was boarding with Line, a woman who worked as a secretary at the rink. She and her family lived beside the center and I stayed there during the week and went home on the weekends. I was sharing a room with another girl. In the evening, after Lloyd's classes, she and I would sit on the bunk beds and rub a smelly muscle relaxant on each other's legs. We couldn't even walk up the stairs because our calves were so sore! Line said she knew when we had aerobics because she could smell the ointment when she went to bed at night.

We took the classes a couple of times a week. Lloyd was determined to get us in shape: he wouldn't let up. The sessions were set to music, and to this day when I hear the song that we used to do jumping jacks to—and I mean hundreds of them at a time—I can't stand to listen to it because it reminds me of those stupid jumping jacks and the pain I endured for days after.

Lloyd

When Isabelle and I began skating together, we didn't have problems because, quite simply, we couldn't communicate. In fact, in the beginning, it was as if I was skating with Josée because she made all the decisions for Isabelle and nothing was done without Josée's approval.

Each session began with a lesson and most of the details would be worked out during that time. Things were a little easier because all the pairs elements have English names, so we would say the name of the element and then perform it. We also communicated through hand gestures. Although I wasn't nervous about throwing her, I did have to think about making every throw smaller because of her size. We had to work on that for years before we mastered it.

It took me a couple of months to get back in shape but, as I've mentioned, there was no off-ice training to speak of at the center and everything was left up to me. It was very different from Preston where we were so regimented. Isabelle and I weren't really training in the beginning, though; we were concentrating more on learning to skate as a team and putting all the elements together. Our schedule was casual. We skated for only three hours a day, since Isabelle was still going to school. I was usually at the rink by 11:00 a.m. and home by 5:00 or 6:00.

We had been skating together only a few weeks when we had to stop to allow Isabelle to practice for the upcoming Nationals in February. She was going to compete in the singles event and I intended to be there to root for her. But, to tell you the truth, I was having mixed feelings about attending the Canadian championships that year. It was the first time that I was going as a spectator and not a participant. I was also a little apprehensive about seeing Mr. Leitch and all my old friends from his school.

Isabelle

When I first began skating with Lloyd, I found it to be different from skating with my old partner. I had been with Pascal so long that we knew exactly what the other was doing, without even speaking. We could communicate through our eyes and by the feel of each other physically out on the ice, especially through our hands. If Pascal was going to add or take out a crosscut for example, I would instinctively be aware of it. We just always knew where the other was going.

I couldn't do that for a long time with Lloyd because it takes years to develop that kind of sense with a partner. In the beginning, if Lloyd and I were going into the corners and our pattern wasn't the same, I'd be wondering, Is he going to do an extra crosscut? Oops . . . he did and I didn't.

But, in so many ways, Lloyd and Pascal were very much alike. They both knew where they wanted to go and how to get there. They also didn't like being told what to do and were extremely confident about their skating ability. Their attitude was, I know I can do it and will do it when it is time, so let's not work too hard right now. They were laid back about practicing, whereas I firmly believe that practice makes perfect. If I do something over and over again, I know I will be able to perform it correctly in competition. They would do an element once before an event and believed the competition itself would pull them up to perform it again there. Lloyd and Pascal shared another habit that I never could figure out. They chewed on their fingers—not their fingernails, their *fingers*. I don't know what I did that drove both of my partners to this particular habit but I suppose it must have been me. It was just too much of a coincidence to be anything else!

I quickly discovered that, with my new partner, I wasn't really afraid of the throws or of anything else. In fact, I thought all the elements we were performing technically were cool. I actually liked doing them and looked forward to practice.

I was once again enjoying the pure exhilaration of my sport and didn't feel like competing on my own at Nationals. I didn't want to skate singles anymore and had only done it because I'd been without a partner and had nothing else to do. Josée talked me into going on with it. As she said, it would probably be my first and only experience competing on my own. Lloyd and I stopped our pairs training two weeks before Nationals so I could concentrate on skating singles. But I just couldn't pay attention to singles when I was skating so well in pairs with Lloyd. Josée had to actually kick him out of the rink for those two weeks. I spent the time freeskating by myself and sorely missing the excitement of pairs.

Lloyd

It was tough going to the 1987 Nationals in Ottawa. Being there only to watch left me with an empty feeling. I ran into my old buddies from Preston and immediately noticed that they had a totally different attitude toward me than when I had last seen them. Many people wouldn't even talk to me. I discovered from a good friend that Mr. Leitch had told all the kids not to speak to me. He had informed them that I was no longer part of the group and that he didn't want them hanging around me, explaining that I was a bad person. My friend ultimately got in trouble with Mr. Leitch for defying him and speaking to me. My old coach later denied this but I was there when other skaters had left him and he had issued the same order.

I had always maintained that, when I saw him again, I would go out of my way to say, "Hello. How are you?" But when I greeted him at Nationals, he walked right by, as if I wasn't there. If someone else was around, he acknowledged me with a curt "Hi," because it wouldn't have looked good to others to snub me. But if it was just him and me, he wouldn't speak to me at all.

I was prepared for this reception, though. As I've said, I had seen him do it to others and knew what was going to happen. Was I angry? Absolutely not. To this day, I've never had bad feelings toward him. I understood where he was coming from, having been with him too long not to understand. I know what Mr. Leitch did for me and that will never change.

People were finding out that Isabelle and I had teamed up, and although no one said anything to me, I sensed their apprehension. I am sure everyone believed she was too small to be my partner and was going to end up hurt. When they asked how it was going, I told them that I was having a good time, enjoying the experience, and that we were skating very well.

When the pairs competition was up, I watched it with more than casual interest. I carefully judged who would be our competition next year and concluded that Isabelle and I would definitely be in that group. Others may not have thought so but I knew it beyond a doubt.

Isabelle

I think many people were negative when Lloyd and I became partners and really didn't expect anything to come of it. They thought Lloyd was too big, too old and too stubborn for me. I believe, in their opinion, I was just this little person who didn't speak up much—the type that wouldn't say "Boo!" to a fly. I think people thought it wouldn't work because they felt Lloyd was too strong a personality. He would control me forever.

Their reactions didn't bother me. I am not the type of person to worry about those things or take them to heart. As long as I was skating, I didn't care and tried my hardest every day. It was true in the beginning that Lloyd took control of our team but he had no more control than Josée had. That was fine with me. I am a follower anyway and don't like to boss people around.

Because Lloyd was so much older and had all the experience, every now and then there would be a struggle between him and my coaches. They tended to treat me the same way they did when I was skating with Pascal and insisted on our performing moves repeatedly.

That didn't usually sit well with Lloyd and we had to cut back on repetitions.

If any conflict did arise, I would side with the coaches and this continued for the first three years that Lloyd and I were together. I had been with them so long and they knew how to treat me to get my best possible performance. It would have been almost impossible for me to stand up to them at that time in my life. Nor did I want to; I believed they knew what was best for me.

I did notice every now and then that Josée or Eric would comment on something that Mr. Leitch may or may not have done at his school. When this happened, Lloyd would inevitably tell them not to make comparisons with Mr. Leitch. He would say, "This is how you teach and I agree with it but I liked the way Mr. Leitch taught as well. You both have different methods so I'd rather not hear anything about Mr. Leitch." If one of the kids said something negative about my partner's old coach, such as, "I would never go to his school," Lloyd would answer, "Well you don't know what it is like there, so don't say that." He would stand up for Mr. Leitch but Lloyd is that type of person. He has so much respect for people who looked out for him and showed him they cared. He will always respect and care for those people, no matter what.

Lloyd

I had no problems dealing with Josée and Eric and actually found Josée to be very much like Mr. Leitch. Although those two probably don't see any similarities, they really are alike. This is evident in their on-ice teaching mentalities and their demand for respect from their students. Where they differ is in their off-ice attitudes. Josée and Isabelle had and still have a wonderful relationship off the ice. Josée is very good at separating the two areas and was great friends with all her students, whereas Mr. Leitch believed that no coach should fraternize with a skater at any time.

When I first left Mr. Leitch, I made the decision that I would never again be ruled as I was under him. I would not allow anyone to say that it was their way or no way and expect me to follow complacently. My mind had been made up before I left Ontario and, from then on, I was going to have input and speak my mind. I had resolved that if I didn't think something was being done properly, I would say so.

There was conflict between Josée and me right from the start because we both wanted control. I believed then, as I do now, that I knew more about pairs skating than Josée and Eric would ever know but I didn't understand how to manage everything. For example, I didn't know how Isabelle would react in certain situations. I needed them and they needed me, but as for the technical side of pairs skating, they weren't going to teach me anything new.

Josée was always trying to alter my way of doing things; coaches always think their way is better. I wasn't about to change because I knew what I was doing was correct. We had many disagreements in the first while because I came from Mr. Leitch's school, which was considered to be the powerhouse at the time. Josée would make comments such as, "Well, at *this* school, we do it this way. At Mr. Leitch's school, they may have done it that way but we don't."

For the first couple of months, we argued about comments like that until I put my foot down and said, "Look, I am here because I want to be here. I don't want you to say anything else about Mr. Leitch or his school. I am very proud of where I came from, so don't knock it down or I am leaving. I don't want to hear you mention Mr. Leitch again."

Periodically over the next two or three years, his name would crop up and I would get angry. We would argue and I'd stay away for a couple of days and then go back and say, "If you are going to continue to bring it up, I'm going to continue to blast you because, in my mind, it is over. It is done with. I am here and, please, let's not do this anymore."

In all the years that I have been with Josée and Eric, I have never learned anything that I didn't already know. Yes, I was taught different ways of doing things. But all of my knowledge of skating came from being with Mr. Leitch for those fifteen years.

Off the ice, though, Eric and Josée were very nice. I suppose it was like any situation at the beginning. Things are wonderful because everyone is treating each other with kid gloves, and that first year we were still going through the "honeymoon" period. The only problems we had in the beginning occurred on the ice, when they would say that their way was better than Mr. Leitch's—something I couldn't tolerate.

Isabelle

I have to admit that for the first few months I found the language barrier between Lloyd and me to be almost insurmountable. Luckily, the technical words are the same in English and French, but to explain anything that was complicated, we had to go to Josée.

In spite of our communication problems, Lloyd and I strived to become friends by taking the time to ask each other questions about our personal lives and how we were feeling about things. We still do that. And in the beginning, although our conversations were extremely limited, I was slowly learning English. I was so intent on explaining what I was feeling to him that I would get angry at myself for not being able to say exactly what I wanted. I would go home at night and try to study but found it very difficult. My brain was too tired after skating because I had been working so hard to communicate with Lloyd in English. It was like . . . Please, don't make me think anymore! It was a type of stress but I could really feel it and wasn't able to concentrate on much else. When I got home, I didn't want to hear any English but then I was even getting mixed up with French as well.

This struggle went on for at least six months. But it was funny because during the time I was learning English and Lloyd was trying to understand French, we developed a special language between the two of us. For example, I would come up with a word such as "deconcentrate," which doesn't mean anything in English but to me meant, "I am not concentrating properly." Lloyd would understand what I was trying to say and wouldn't bother to correct me. I would try to explain words to Lloyd and say them half in French and half in English and this way we began to understand each other.

Today, if I say a word like "deconcentrate," Lloyd answers, "Oh yeah," because he knows what I mean and won't tell me I'm wrong. But then I'll say in public, "I'm deconcentrating," and when people ask me what I mean, I'll explain, proudly thinking that I know what I am talking about. At times like these, I can't figure out why Lloyd can understand me and they can't.

It is the same with the letter *h*, which I don't pronounce. Lloyd doesn't bother correcting that anymore. He just understands what I am trying to say and we get on with it.

Lloyd

Although Isabelle and I did our best to communicate while we were skating, once we got off the ice we usually went our separate ways. That first year we didn't develop much of a relationship apart from skating. I thought of her as a little kid and she spent most of her time studying or with her parents.

During the first few months, most of my spare time was spent getting back into shape. I also passed many solitary hours at Josée and Eric's, skiing or listening to music and reflecting on whether or not I was doing the right thing. I still wondered if I had made the right decision. Should I be here? This question was going through my mind all the time.

I am not the type that gets homesick while I'm away. I also didn't miss Mr. Leitch and his school but I was lonely for some of my friends and I spent much time writing letters or calling them. I also tried to go home almost every weekend to see some of my closer friends, leaving Montreal on a Friday and driving back Sunday.

Whenever I could, I would sit down with Josée and Eric and ask them questions about Isabelle. What is she really like? What does she need? I thought knowing these things would help us communicate on the ice through movement. We often spent many hours

(left) Lloyd at six months.

(below) Lloyd at age three.

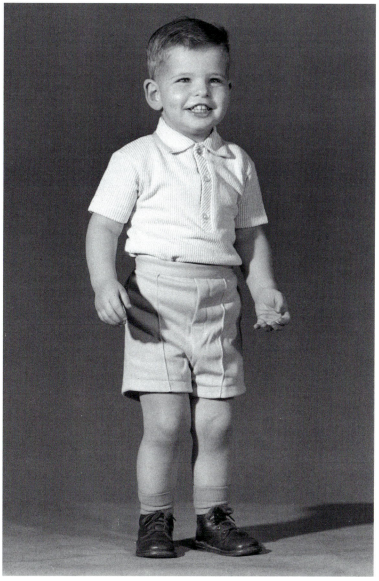

(above left)
Lloyd and Joan Sills
in 1971.

(above right)
From left: Dave McLlwain
(who now plays for the
Pittsburg Penquins), his
brother Mark McLlwain,
Joanne Whitman and
Lloyd at the Seaforth
Carnival Awards: Lloyd
received the trophy for
the most advanced skater.

(left)
Lloyd and his first partner,
Lorri Baier, as Novice
National Champions in
1977: both age fourteen.

(above left) Isabelle and her brother Dominique at ages two and five.
(above right) Isabelle at age four.

Isabelle, Dominique and her dad playing hockey in Kingsbury in 1974.

(above left) Isabelle at age four: a ballerina.
(above right) Isabelle in her "pizza box" hat: her first show in 1976.

Isabelle (age ten) and Pascal Courchesne at Provincials in 1980.

(above left) Isabelle and Lloyd as "Betty and Al": their first show number, in 1988.
(above right) Lloyd and Kurt Browning at the 1989 World Championships in Paris.

Dominique, Isabelle, Dominique's wife, Josée and Lloyd in Halifax, in 1990.

(above) Isabelle, Lloyd, Sergei Grinkov, Ekaterina Gordeeva, Artur Dmitriev, Natalia Mishkutenok at World's 1990 in Halifax.
Photo: Athlete Information Bureau

(left) Lloyd and Isabelle performing the split triple twist at the 1991 World's.
Photo: Gérard Châtaigneau

(above left) Isabelle and Josée Chouinard having fun on the 1991 World Tour in Europe.
(above right) Lloyd and Todd Sand on the 1991 World Tour in Europe: no hot water in Italy.

Lloyd and Martin Smith at the Park Restaurant, Chicago on the 1991 World Tour.

Opening Ceremonies in Albertville, 1992. From left to right: Lloyd Eisler,
Doug Ladret, Elvis Stojko, Kris Wirtz, Mark Janoshak, Kurt Browning.

(above left) Opening Ceremonies, Albertville Olympics, 1992:
Lloyd, Isabelle, Josée Picard. (above right) Lloyd tries to console
Isabelle after their short program in Albertville in 1992.

discussing where we saw the year going and how Isabelle and I needed to mold our styles so we would fit each other better.

Isabelle

Lloyd and I didn't see each other at all as friends outside of the rink that first year. I was in my last year of high school in the Study and Sport program, which took up much of my time. When I wasn't doing homework or skating, I liked to hang out with my own friends, who were a lot younger than Lloyd. Often, I would read by myself or relax with my parents, doing things together as a family.

Although I was boarding, my parents would often come and get me during the week and I went home to St-Jean on the weekends. Mom and Dad were happy that I was skating with Lloyd but they were a little afraid because he was so much older. I don't think it was a big concern for them after they got to know him.

My dad still came to the rink at least once a week because he was very much involved in my career. I soon discovered that he and Lloyd were both strong willed. Because they were similar in personality, every now and then they would go head to head and it took a few years for them to calm down around each other. I mean, it was stupid. They wanted the same goals to be achieved; they just didn't realize it. I knew it, yet it took a long time for them to realize it. But that first year wasn't too bad and Lloyd even went to work for my father at his company. Dad wanted to make sure my partner had enough money to see him through.

Lloyd

At the beginning of the summer, I decided to move out of Eric and Josée's chalet and rent an apartment in St-Jean, which was only thirty minutes from the rink. I don't like living with other people and wanted to be on my own. Josée and Eric had been charging me $50 a week to cover room and board. They were fantastic about it and never complained but I felt it was time to move on.

I decided St-Jean was the best place to live because Isabelle's father had offered me a job as an assistant to the mechanic at his tire plant. My shift ran from 5:00 p.m. until midnight, after we had skated all day. But I needed the money. I had spent almost my entire savings and was far too proud to ask my parents, who weren't funding my skating anymore. That job got me through, month to month, and paid my rent and basic expenses. Unfortunately, I didn't have enough money to cover all my expenses, including the $32 per hour coaching fee, which was charged by Josée and Eric and split between Isabelle and me.

Throughout this period, I was never able to pay Josée and Eric all that I owed. If their fee was $500 for the month, I may have only been able to give $300 and so I constantly owed them money. Josée and Eric were very good about it. They understood and told me that, when I finally made it, I could pay them back whatever I wasn't able to afford then.

I was grateful to Isabelle's father for giving me the job. He was deeply involved in Isabelle's career and seemed to be at the rink four or five days a week. Her mom was very nice and always so polite but tended to stay in the background. You could see that it was Isabelle's dad who made the decisions. When we first started skating, I believe Gill was afraid of me because I was so much bigger than his daughter and had a reputation for being too outspoken and being my own person. That wasn't acceptable in our sport and I sensed his trepidation. But in the beginning we got along well because Isabelle and I hadn't started training seriously. We were just skating every day and trying new things and there weren't many decisions to be made. Once we started putting it all together, her dad would step in with his opinions, but he wasn't involved too much in the decision-making process that first year.

I think it took Gill a while to get used to me. As a matter of fact, it took everyone a while. I remember, when the first warm weather came, I went home for a couple of weeks to pick up my motorcycle and drive it back to Montreal. Deciding I had better let everyone know I had returned, I went over to the arena, dressed in leather and wearing a bandanna and sunglasses. I don't think I had shaved in ten days. I was standing at the side of the rink and couldn't figure out why nobody came over to say hello. They all seemed to be ignoring me. I thought, What the hell is going on?

My partner skated by and I said, "Hi, Isabelle," and the look on her face said: Who is that guy saying hello to me? Do I know him? Does he know me? Then it struck me that she and everyone else hadn't recognized me. Everyone, including Josée and Eric, was staring at me as if to say, Who is that guy over there and why is he in the arena? Isabelle continued to look at me shyly and then cautiously skated over to me, recognizing me only after I had removed my head gear.

I am sure Josée was shocked because she placed as much importance on outward appearance as Mr. Leitch did. Both Isabelle and I had been brought up the same way. Seeing me like that was probably a little scary for her but that school of thought, with respect to appearances, never really clicked with me.

Isabelle

In a rink, everybody knows everyone else; all the parents, family and friends are familiar with each other. So when someone steps into the arena, you know that person and everyone is comfortable around one another.

One day, after Lloyd had been away a while, he came into the center. We all looked at each other, wondering who he was. He had grown a beard and wore leather pants, a leather jacket, sunglasses, and some sort of head gear. I think it's called a bandanna. He was at ice level and the kids got scared and asked what this guy was doing here. I skated by and he said, "Hi, Isabelle." I didn't answer and hurried over to one of my friends and whispered, "He knows me!"

By this time, Lloyd had taken off his bandanna and sunglasses and I slowly approached him. I skated closer and closer and when it finally dawned on me who it was, I yelled, "Oh, my God! I thought you were a stranger!" Funny, we had been skating together a few months by that time and I didn't even recognize him.

Lloyd

Come spring, after the national and world championships, people at the CFSA started to take an interest in us. Prior to that, they hadn't said much in response to Josée and Eric's pushing them to come and take a look at us. Our coaches were very positive about the situation, but in the first few months of a skating year, the CFSA is too busy with Nationals and Worlds. It is not the time to be looking at new teams or skaters because there is so much going on.

Once competitions were over, we had a couple of monitoring sessions, where they came to watch us. I had never apologized to anyone from the CFSA for my comments the year before but I believe Mr. Leitch had calmed the waters for me a bit.

Isabelle and I began to get our programs together but we didn't perform a summer competition that year. Our first one as a team wasn't until October, when we were to go to Czechoslovakia to compete in Prague Skate. As we began to prepare for this competition, we soon found there was a problem with the way Isabelle and I were used to training.

Isabelle trains through repetition. I, on the other hand, like to do something once and that is it. So we had a lot of difficulties because Josée and Eric taught like Mr. Leitch: to them, more is better. I would say, "No, I am not doing it." Many fights developed from this because they would insist, "You *are* going to do it again," and I would refuse. They would then declare, "You have to!" Being stubborn, I would answer, "No, I don't have to do anything. We are *not* doing it again." So we got into many arguments while training for this competition and Isabelle often felt stuck in the middle because she didn't know who to side with. It must have been hard for her because Josée and Eric had been her coaches for many years, yet I was her partner. I often felt sorry for Isabelle during those times because I understood her dilemma.

Isabelle

I wasn't used to Lloyd's way of training and found that we had to compromise to keep the peace. Instead of doing something many times, as I wanted to, or only once, as he wanted to, we would do it twice. Actually, Lloyd's way helped me because I learned that I could do something when I had to.

We didn't argue too much in that first year. The big fights came later. It took us about five months to have our first argument and it was really funny. I don't even remember what we disagreed about, it could have been because I kept missing a jump. But I still wasn't bilingual enough to fight in English. I argued in French and he started to laugh at me and that only made me angrier. So I yelled at him in French and he laughed even harder. I think he thought of me as a little sister. I know I was certainly beginning to feel as if he was my big brother and enjoyed the fact that we were getting closer. By then, we understood each other well enough that if I was having a problem, he was the one I turned to for advice.

In the beginning, Lloyd would tell me that he wanted to skate only one session a day. If I or my coaches insisted on two sessions, he would reluctantly agree. One day he called to tell me he was sick and couldn't go to the rink. He would call once every three weeks at least, saying he was ill. This went on for a few months and then, one day, I suddenly realized what game he was playing. So, the next time he phoned, I headed over to his apartment before I went to the rink. I knocked on the door and when he answered he had a look of complete surprise on his face. "What are you doing here?" he asked. I said, "I wanted to see if you were actually sick because, if you are not, you can come and skate with me." He didn't have much of a choice because he obviously wasn't ill. He just didn't feel like skating sometimes. After that, I did this whenever he called and each time Lloyd grudgingly gave in and came to the rink with me.

Mom and Dad were still funding my skating at this time, although I had been carded by the government when I was skating with Pascal. I don't know how much I received because the money went directly to my parents, who paid my bills. Unlike Lloyd, I was fortunate enough not to have to worry about money and never had a part-time job. All of my energy was devoted to skating and school.

Lloyd

My good friend John Thomas choreographed both of the programs that we were to skate for the upcoming competition and the rest of the year. The short program was called "Two Tribes Go to War" and it was a great piece of music. Our long was a medley of songs by the Beatles. John had been working with Josée and Eric before I got there and it was fun having him make up the programs. It was very easy to listen to him and we talked a lot about old times while we were developing our routines.

By that first competition, the CFSA started carding us, so we would be receiving money from the government through the association, retroactive to the beginning of the fiscal year, which was April 1. Isabelle and I were carded as C-1 athletes, whereas I had last been carded as an A athlete. This meant that I wasn't getting as much money as before; we each received only $350 a month. But some money was better than no money and I couldn't wait for my first check to arrive.

For Thanksgiving, Pam and John drove down to spend the weekend with me at my apartment, which must have been all of twenty by thirty feet. It was tiny and they couldn't believe the way I was living to make ends meet. But we had a big Thanksgiving dinner, complete with a turkey. That year, Pam and John played a big role in keeping my spirits up when my career was at a crucial point.

Josée, Eric and I were having a lot of difficulty preparing for the competition in Prague because we had never before traveled together. They were new coaches to me—I didn't know what to expect from them and they didn't know what to expect from me. Before a competition, I get a little stressed and so I work harder. Because I am a perfectionist, the slightest mistake will agitate me. Overall, it was a real learning experience for us to go to this competition. It didn't help that I was also upset because I was preparing to go to Czechoslovakia but had run out of funds.

I hadn't received my carding check from the CFSA yet and I was down to my last $20, which was all I had to travel with. How I was going to pay the rent when I returned, I had no idea. I refused to ask my parents for help and the situation was very stressful for me. Going to an international competition was a big break for Isabelle and me, yet I had no money and didn't know how I was going to live when I got back.

We left for Czechoslovakia and stopped for a two-hour layover in Toronto, where Pam and John met me at the airport. I had secretly confided my money problems to John and, the next thing I knew, Pam had gone to the bank and withdrawn $100 to give to me. Well, I knew that at the time they weren't well off either and it was probably the last $100 they had. But Pam made me take the money and I was very touched by my friends' generosity.

After arriving in Czechoslovakia, Isabelle and I spent the week practicing and the sessions seemed to go very well. Only Josée had come with us—and it would be that way for most of our future events. I did feel anxious, however, because this was our first competition together and we were still feeling each other out. What was Isabelle going to do? What was I going to do? What was Josée going to do? How were we going to react to each other's judgment?

All in all, though, the week went great. Isabelle and I were getting along fine and spent a lot of time together off the ice. We ate together, decided on what to wear together and left for the rink together. It was this competition that marked the beginning of my trying to look after Isabelle. After all, I was older and I think everyone expected this of me. I took her under my wing, introducing her to everyone and spent as much time as possible with her, instead of letting her fend for herself.

During the competition, we skated very well and placed third, overall. We might have been able to place higher but we were still pleased with how we had skated. Isabelle landed her first double

Axel in competition, which was a highlight for her. It definitely gave us a boost and carried us for the next six months. It was at that point that I stopped second-guessing myself and finally realized that I had made the right decision.

On the way home, I stopped in Toronto and saw Pam and John. I had bought them a little crystal vase with some of the money they had loaned me. I was very excited about how Isabelle and I had skated but was still worried about how I was going to pay my rent when I arrived home. Luckily, the check from the CFSA was waiting for me and I was able to pay some bills. But I realized this situation couldn't continue, so I contacted an organization called the Bursary Fund.

This excellent group funds skaters and the money is not expected to be paid back. It used to be available only for kids from Ontario, although this has since changed. I went to Jim Irving, the person in charge at the time, and said, "I have been skating for the Bursary for a long time and I could really use some funding just to get me through this year." I had always skated the Bursary, which is a two-day show and dinner usually held in Toronto at the Granite or Cricket Club. At the time of this writing, I have missed only one Bursary in nineteen years.

Jim considered my request and soon I received some money from them. Thanks to the Bursary Fund, I was able to survive until the end of the season and I will always be grateful to them. In fact, for the last couple of years Isabelle and I have skated the Bursary Fund Dinner as professionals for free, to repay them for their generosity to me and other skaters.

When my parents found out about my dire financial situation, they really gave it to me because I hadn't asked them for money. But I explained to my mother, "Well, you weren't in support of me when I left and I wasn't going to bow down and ask if I could borrow some money to go away with." Dad was very angry, telling me that they would always stand behind me. He made me promise not to leave for a competition under those circumstances again, without first coming to him.

Isabelle

Lloyd and I were about to compete for the first time and it was to be an international event at that. We were happy with our programs, although they both tended to be rather technical. They weren't very artistic and didn't have much flow. It was all elements, elements, elements.

We were nervous because it was our first time away together. Josée accompanied us and, as always, I was happy she was there. Immediately before competition, I feel anxious, and the more anxious I get, the more my body feels heavy, especially my feet. I feel weighted down. Sometimes I believe I won't make it through the number, thinking, How am I ever going to do the last jump if I am so tired after the first one? Then, during the performance, I will start thinking, I know I am going to fall; I'm too tired. Josée's personality tends to lift me up; she bounces around, telling me about her shopping and this and that. Suddenly, I start to feel lighter. By the time I get on the ice, I know I am ready. When you feel light and quick, it is easy to make the jumps.

Lloyd really looked after me at this competition. He would have lunch with us, just to make sure I was eating, and he constantly asked me if everything was all right. He even went shopping with Josée and me a few times.

We skated pretty well during the competition and came in third. A couple of things happened during the long program that made me realize just how comfortable we were getting with each other.

The program had three throws in it and in one of them Lloyd had a key word that he would say to me. The word was "wait" and in practice he always spoke it in English. During the competition, Lloyd said the key word, but he said it in French. I thought, Huh? I landed the jump but it really surprised me. Three-quarters of the way through the program, we stopped, and the fast music was supposed to begin but we were ahead of ourselves. This is why we had been nervous to begin with because it is this type of situation where, unless you are really familiar with your partner, you are not sure how they will react. Lloyd said to me, "Stop. Bring your arms in and turn." So I did what he said and it never appeared as if we didn't know what we were doing. We matched perfectly and then continued along with the music. It felt good that we were starting to get used to each other.

On the morning we were to leave Prague, we had to catch a bus that was leaving at 5:00 a.m. Although Lloyd assured us he would be there, he didn't wake up and he missed the bus. Josée and I had his skate bag and we were really mad. We just couldn't believe that he would miss the bus at our first competition. He barely made the flight, as well. It was a pain to us because we had been so worried about him.

When we returned home, we began to prepare for Divisionals. Because we had participated in an international competition just prior to Sectionals, we didn't have to compete in that category. It is believed if you are good enough to go to an international event, you are good enough to have a buy at Sectionals.

Lloyd and I skated well at Divisionals and, for the first time, I really believed we had a chance to be up there with the top people at Nationals. Our competitors were Hough and Ladret and Johnston and Benning, all excellent skaters. Could we do it? Were my childhood dreams about to come true?

Lloyd

That competition gave us the mental go-ahead that we needed to get to Nationals that year. Isabelle and I returned from Prague and, in early December, we were off to Divisionals in Gatineau. It was there that many people seemed to suddenly realize that we were skating together and began to talk about us . . . "Brasseur and Eisler . . . you should see them. They can do this and they can do that!" Everyone from the CFSA came as well and it was exciting to realize they were here to watch Isabelle and me.

After Prague, I think the CFSA thought we had potential but I believe that at the Divisionals, where we skated phenomenally, they sat up and took notice. Josée and Eric quickly stepped in, though, and told us not to let the CFSA's interest throw us off our plan of attack for the year. They stressed, "We have done very well up to this point. We have trained properly and gone the right distance with the right measures. Because they think you are doing well, they are going to start interfering. Don't let them change what you have been doing for the last ten months." Isabelle and I took this advice seriously and didn't sway from our path.

My partner and I were getting along wonderfully. Isabelle was learning more English and we were starting to communicate better. But Eric, Josée and I continued to have disagreements because, although we had the same goals, we had different views on how to achieve them. This was, of course, because we were still unfamiliar with one another and trying to get used to each other's ways. At this point in time, we were disagreeing on just about everything and arguments ensued about how we should train, how we should work, what we should wear, when we should do things and when we shouldn't do things. It was a constant learning phase for all of us.

I went home for Christmas and I noticed that my mom was less negative about my continuing to skate. In fact, she took a real interest and asked me a lot of questions about how I was doing and whether it was working out. We had done well at Prague and Divisionals, and although there was excitement about our skating, some people still didn't believe we could succeed at Nationals. Both my parents told me that, since we had made it this far, they believed we would do well at the Canadian championships. There was no question our competition was going to be tough but I, like my parents, believed we could do it. We just had to ride the momentum that had carried us this far.

CHAPTER FOUR

Proving Ourselves

Lloyd

THE WEATHER in Victoria was beautiful for the 1988 Nationals. Considering that it was late January and we had left Montreal in a deep freeze, it was a pleasant surprise. Although the entire Quebec team always traveled together, I still wasn't familiar with many of the other skaters and so Isabelle and I spent most of our time with each other or our parents.

Stress seemed to be running high that week but Isabelle and I were feeling good. We had been skating well and figured we had nothing to lose and everything to gain. Our plan was to go out and show people who had written us off as a mismatch that they were wrong. We had done hundreds and hundreds of run-throughs and believed our two programs to be very good, with a high degree of difficulty.

I was a touch more excited than Isabelle to be at this particular Nationals. Having missed them the year before, I wanted to prove to the skating world that I had made the right choice in leaving Mr. Leitch and teaming up with Isabelle. I knew beyond a shadow of a doubt that my decision had been the right one but it was the first time that we would be seen together at the national level. I was looking forward to showing everyone what we could do.

Since this was an Olympic year, to make the team we would have to compete against some of Canada's finest pairs skaters, including Doug Ladret and Christine Hough (Tuffy), and Lyndon Johnston and Denise Benning. I had skated with both these teams when I had been with Mr. Leitch and I knew how good they were. Doug and Tuffy had been to Worlds the year before and Lyndon and Denise were currently ranked fifth. As far as my old coach was concerned, I wasn't too worried about seeing him again but I still felt a deep loss. We hadn't spoken and so, of course, nothing had been resolved between us.

At Nationals, the pairs competition is usually held on the Thursday and Friday and Isabelle and I would arrive on the previous Sunday. We were staying at the stately Empress Hotel and were pleased that our parents were able to make the trip. It was the first time that they would see us together at a major competition. My mom and Isabelle's dad were like two peas in a pod as they both fretted about how we would do. However, Dad and Claudette, also alike in personality, calmed them down by saying, "Oh, just let them go and don't worry. They will be fine." I was glad they were there for each other because my mind was on how much work we had to do and what I wanted us to accomplish at this event.

Isabelle

People seemed to be curious about us before the Canadian championships. It was an Olympic year and everyone was eager to discover who would be on the team. I think they were also wondering how we would do under pressure.

Lloyd and I were feeling good, though. We thought we had a chance to make it to the Olympics by doing well at this competition but I tried not to think about it. I had to keep my mind on skating and I also wanted to enjoy myself. It was the first time we were skating together at a national event and I was nervous about the outcome.

I was glad that my parents were able to come. It had been a year of ups and downs as Lloyd and I worked everything out, and I wanted to show them what we could do at a competition of this status. Both Eric and Josée were also with us since so many of their kids were entered in Nationals at the junior level. As a matter of fact, Julie Marcotte, who is a very close friend and who currently does the choreography for our fast numbers, came in second at junior dance that year. But what I really thought was great was how Lloyd took care of me. We had breakfast and lunch together and he made sure that I was happy and at ease in my surroundings. He was wonderful.

Lloyd

On the first day of practice, I saw Mr. Leitch, who acknowledged my greeting with only a quick hello before walking past me. That was our entire conversation for the week but I knew he was not the type to easily forget. It was something I just had to learn to live with.

It was nice to talk to the other skaters who I hadn't seen in a while, especially Tuffy and Doug, and I noticed that aside from the other competitors, there were many people, including the judges, who came to see our practices. I guess because we had taken the Divisionals by storm, we had created a stir. At any rate, Isabelle and I felt the pressure to perform well at practices under their watchful eyes. Josée and Eric also pushed us a bit harder because they wanted to show that their team was a contender, so each practice was well scoped out beforehand.

Prior to competition, all teams meet to draw the order of skating. The officials literally put your names in a hat, pull them out and you skate in the order in which they are drawn. At this particular Nationals, all of us thought the draw was a big joke. There were probably between nine and twelve senior teams and usually the better skaters are spread throughout the competition. But, this time, the first teams drawn were Tuffy and Doug, Isabelle and me and Denise and Lyndon—the top three. After the draw we looked at each other and said, "Yeah, right." It seemed a little too convenient that we were all in the same warm-up and skating one right after another. Obviously, we could be compared very easily, skating in this order.

On the day of our short program, I followed my routine of coming into practice, seeing my parents and then spending the rest of the day alone. Our programs were the same as those we had skated in Prague. Apart from minor revisions, our long and short numbers usually stay the same throughout the skating season, and although I loved them that year, I absolutely hated my outfit for the short program. It can only be described as ugly, ugly, ugly. It was fuchsia from top to bottom and I detested it from the day I tried it on. Just before our competition, I was in the dressing room getting into my costume. Everyone looked at me and someone sarcastically commented, "Hey, nice color!" They didn't have to tell *me.* I knew it was disgusting and the only reason I agreed to wear it was that out on the ice it looked half decent.

Tuffy and Doug were first up in the short program and they skated clean. Then it was our turn and, much to our excitement, we skated perfectly. We came off the ice absolutely ecstatic and waited for our marks. They came up and—boom—we were ahead of Tuffy and Doug. We sat and watched Denise and Lyndon skate and, unfortunately, they didn't do well. By the time all twelve teams had skated, Isabelle and I had finished in first place! Everyone was stunned. We had only competed together in one Divisionals and one international competition and here we were, beating the team that was fifth in the world! We were thrilled and our coaches and parents were on cloud nine.

Isabelle

There was no one happier than Lloyd and me after we skated so well in the short program. But because I had put all my energy into it, the next morning, at our practice for the long, I couldn't do anything. Our parents were watching us and cringing each time I fell. After a while, I got back on my feet and I knew I would be okay that night. Even though I had a bad practice, I still felt comfortable about everything. We had been skating well before we left and there was no reason for me to believe that wouldn't continue. I knew our parents were unhappy about the practice but I was calm and believed I would do just fine in the competition.

Lloyd

The top teams after the original program always skate in the last group during the technical competition. We also practice together on the last day, which is different from the rest of the week, when teams usually practice individually. Isabelle and I didn't have a great practice that day; it wasn't bad but it certainly was not our best.

I recall going back to my room after practice and relaxing as I usually do, while Isabelle went out with her mom and dad. It came time for the competition and we had a fairly good warm-up that was also fun because Doug and I were kidding with each other on the ice. We had been friends for a long time and always got along famously. Both of us were happy to be sitting in first and second place.

Lyndon, on the other hand, was very cool toward me. I think it bothered him that he and Denise had been the top team coming into Nationals and they were now sitting in third place. I also know that he was one of the people who thought I had made a huge mistake by leaving Mr. Leitch and I could definitely feel the tension in the air.

We had drawn last to skate; Lyndon and Denise drew first. Again they didn't skate well but Tuffy and Doug gave a good performance. It was finally our turn and Isabelle and I skated very well. At that point in our career, we probably couldn't have done any better. The marks were tallied and it was close, with Tuffy and Doug winning by the score of only one judge. We had three firsts and they had four out of seven scores. But I was happy for my friends. It was to be their first and only Canadian championship and they were so excited and such nice people that you couldn't help but be pleased for them. As for Isabelle and me, we were elated to have skated so well. I, personally, was more than a little satisfied to have proven to all those naysayers that they were wrong. We had placed second at our first Nationals and were now off to the Olympics. Amazing!

Isabelle

In those days, you were never sure if you had been chosen for the Olympic team until the last evening of Nationals, when the officials made the formal announcement. Although the top three teams were supposed to go, every now and then they picked the fourth- instead of the third-place team. In 1984, the man who came third had been overlooked and a junior champion was sent to the Olympics in his place. It really wasn't fair to the athletes when this type of favoritism went on. Now, thank goodness, the rules have been changed and only the top skaters are selected. Lloyd and I expected to be chosen but I didn't take it for granted until the announcement was actually made.

I was so excited when our names were called. I was going to my first Olympics and they were to be held in my own country. What a thrill! Something like that rarely happens. My family and coaches couldn't have been happier either. We had always dreamt of the Olympics and now our goals were coming true. We had all worked so hard for this moment and I knew how much Mom, Dad and Dominique had given up for me to get there.

Since we were to perform the same programs at the Olympics, our training didn't change much, but as the time grew nearer, I found myself getting more and more excited. It wasn't nerves, really. I was very young, had nothing to lose and was really just looking forward to the experience.

Something comical happened at one of our practices before the Olympics. I say it is funny now but at the time it was so embarrassing. I was wearing an outfit with a zipper down the front and Lloyd and I were in the sit spin position, facing each other. Suddenly my zipper broke in the middle of the spin! I didn't have anything on underneath. Centrifugal force took over and I couldn't pull my arms in to cover my bare chest. All the while, Lloyd was laughing as I yelled for him to stop. Finally he slowed down but couldn't control his laughter. Josée wanted to know why we had stopped. When she saw my top open, she started to laugh too. I was really red-faced as I fastened it with some safety pins and pulled on a sweater for extra measure.

We arrived in Calgary the second week of February, a week before our event. The short program of the pairs competition always happens the day after the opening ceremony, so we arrived early to get our practice time in. Josée alone accompanied us because, since they had only one team at the Olympics, only one coach was allowed to attend. Both sets of parents came, as well. Labatts had generously offered to fly, for free, two people from each of the Canadian athletes' families and had also arranged to have them billeted at people's homes in Calgary. My parents were told they would be staying with a family by the name of Simonin, and thinking, by the sound of their name, that these people were French, wrote them a letter ahead of time, in French. When Mom and Dad arrived, they discovered their hosts were very English and that they had taken my parents' letter to a French school to have it translated. Raymond and Carol were wonderful to my parents during their stay and I still keep in touch with them.

Lloyd had been telling me before we left what to expect and what to bring with me, so I had packed everything I thought I might require. When we landed in Calgary, we went through security at the airport and then into a huge building to register and pick up our uniforms. I was astonished because they gave me two huge duffel bags of clothing. Everything from ski suits and jackets to long underwear, socks and nylons was stuffed inside those bags. I felt like a kid at Christmas.

When we arrived at the Olympic village, which was actually part of the University of Calgary, we were held up going through accreditation. I didn't mind the delay because I was dreading what was supposed to take place next—the femininity tests. Ever since I had found out that we had made the Olympic team, everyone had been warning me about this particular test, which is held literally to make sure that the women athletes are women.

Other skaters had told me, in quite graphic detail, what to expect and I was petrified! They scared me out of my wits with their stories. Being young and gullible, I believed them, and by the time it was my turn, I had worked myself into a state, preparing for the worst. You can imagine my relief when all I was asked to do was open my mouth, where they took a sample of saliva! Once this was completed, I was given a card that declared me a female and I never had to take the test again.

It seems the teasing I took is a ritual of the Olympics. After all the kidding I had withstood, I figured I had paid my price and made sure this tradition continued with any young female skaters I encountered at the 1992 and 1994 Olympics.

Once inside the village, I was amazed by the size of the facilities. For the two weeks I was there, my mouth was hanging open and my eyes were as big as quarters as I tried to take everything in. The village alone was so large that a person could get lost in it for half a day. There were games and pinball rooms, a movie theater, a bar—everything we could ever want was right there.

On the first night, Lloyd and I decided to go down to the cafeteria for something to eat. Again, I was stunned as I saw hundreds and hundreds of athletes from every country in the world sitting in this massive room. I suddenly felt very tiny and prayed Lloyd wouldn't let go of my hand.

Lloyd

After doing so well at Nationals, people were surprised and cautious in evaluating us. I think they doubted me because I was getting older. They probably thought that I would skate this Olympics and then move on to do something else and that Isabelle wouldn't grow any bigger or stronger. But none of that mattered to my partner or me. We now knew what we could do and figured that the future could only get better.

Josée and Eric seemed to be a little stressed out between Nationals and the Olympics because they wanted us to skate well in this next competition. They pushed us really hard. Eric and I were disagreeing on training habits and techniques, as he and Josée attempted to make our practices more intense. Isabelle and I tried to keep our practices relaxed, since we believed the way we had trained for Nationals had worked. Why change it?

All the pairs skaters traveled together to Calgary, so Tuffy, Doug, Denise, Lyndon, Mr. Leitch, Josée, Isabelle and I were on the same flight. When our plane touched down, we were shuffled onto a security bus and over to registration, which was located in a warehouse on airport property. It was there that we were to pick up our uniforms. We spent about three hours trying on clothing, which consisted of jackets, walking outfits, gloves, sweatpants, track suits, boots, sweaters and countless other items. No one could leave until everyone in our group was fitted. Then we had to load this extra luggage onto the bus and, of course, that took some sorting out. We had each already brought a couple of suitcases and a skate bag and now we had two or three extra pieces to carry.

From there, the bus took us to accreditation, which was held outside the village, where we spent another three hours filling out forms and having our pictures taken, and the girls took their femininity tests. Athletes were coming in at the same time, so there were huge lineups and the process seemed to take forever. Everyone was getting a little cranky because we'd been traveling all day and hadn't eaten and now we had to get back on the bus, which was to take us inside the village. However, the bus was only allowed to come a certain distance from the compound, where it stopped at another security check. At this checkpoint, you put every piece of luggage on a conveyor belt that passed through a metal detector and then you picked up your bags on the other side. From there, it was about a thousand meters to the village and we had to walk the distance, carrying our luggage. Well, you can imagine the scene—several tired, irritated and hungry people, who now have five or six bags each to cope with. The girls obviously couldn't carry them all, so the guys had to make three or four trips between the village and the security entrance. We were not a happy bunch of skaters at that point.

When we finally saw our accommodations, I was surprised. Having been at Sarajevo, where the athletes shared small townhouses that had kitchens, bathrooms and balconies, I guess I was a bit spoiled. In Calgary, we stayed in a dormitory with no private toilet or shower. It was all community living.

I was the odd man out because I didn't have a roommate, so I volunteered to stay with the bobsled team, which had an extra bed. That arrangement was great for me because I knew many of the guys and got along well with them. The rooms were very small, so to make more space we put everything that wasn't necessary in the corridor.

I had a fantastic time with those guys, most of whom I'd met in 1984. Aside from Isabelle, I hardly saw the other skaters, who were staying in a different area of the dorm. That suited me; I could really unwind around the bobsledders because skating usually wasn't the main topic of discussion.

Isabelle

Our practices went well that week and, before I knew it, the day of the opening ceremonies had arrived. How can I describe the feeling I had that day? Obviously, I was excited but the whole scene appeared to be unreal to me. It was a childhood dream come true. When I saw the stadium filled with people, I was spellbound. It was overwhelming and I had a hard time believing that I was really there. All those years, I had glued myself to the television to watch the athletes walk into the stadium at the Olympics, and now it was me marching in!

Lloyd and I were apart for this segment of the ceremonies. I was so little that I was placed at the front. To let you know how small I was, I had to wear running shoes inside my Olympic-issue boots to make them fit!

My parents were somewhere in the audience and I knew they must have been feeling proud as they watched their daughter enter the stadium. Although I had competed at Junior Worlds before and had visited many other countries, I had never experienced a moment like this. I think what impressed me the most was the number of other participants; I just couldn't believe there were that many athletes in the world. When I started to think about all of those who had tried and hadn't made it to the Olympics, I suddenly realized how big the sports world is. I was truly in awe.

Lloyd

The opening ceremonies were fantastic. I remember it being very cold that day and we had just come from a practice. Since Canada was the host country, we were to march in last and had to wait outside forever. But that didn't bother me a bit. It was fun to chat with the other athletes. Some were a little stressed out because they were going to be competing the next day, while others decided not to join the parade, thinking the long walk and cold weather might affect how they trained. But Isabelle and I couldn't wait to march into the stadium.

My partner's excitement was contagious. It was not only her first Olympics but Tuffy's, Doug's and Denise's as well, so it was hard not to get caught up in their enthusiasm. I also thought it was fun to have our coach marching with us. The coaches who are allowed to participate in the march are selected by lottery and Josée had been fortunate enough to be one of them. I think that being in the parade meant a lot to her. We also took great pride in the fact that a skater was to carry the flag and we teased Brian Orser, warning him not to drop it.

When it was finally our turn to walk in, my eyes filled with tears as I heard the roar of the packed stadium. So many athletes I knew had been training for the last four years to make it to the Olympics, and suddenly everything had come together for them and for us and now here we were. It was a very special feeling. It was also wondrous to think that so many Canadians across the country were watching us at that particular moment.

As the ceremonies drew to a close and the cauldron was lit with the symbolic flame, I reflected on the fact that I had actually made it back to the Olympics. It wasn't at all surprising to me. When I decide to do something, I usually work my damnedest to make it happen and, at that moment, I was deeply satisfied that we had made it this far.

Isabelle

The short program was held in the Corral, which seats only 7,000 people. I was used to an arena that size and although I was slightly nervous, we skated very well.

Our parents were sitting side by side, two rows from the front, so I could see them during the competition. Close to the end of our program, the four of them rose to their feet and began cheering as Lloyd yelled to them, "Yes! We did it!"

Lloyd and I felt terrific when it was over and discovered we had finished seventh. Not too bad, considering we'd only been together a year.

Lloyd

For the short program, we had drawn a good position near the end and couldn't have skated any better. When the marks came up, they drew a lot of boos from the crowd. I guess they were protesting the fact that several teams who came ahead of us had fallen and missed elements, and the audience was showing its support to the home team. I wasn't unhappy, though, because I realized it was just the politics of skating. Isabelle and I were new and the judges hadn't seen us before. Our turn would come.

Denise and Lyndon placed fifth, and although Tuffy and Doug skated well, they finished ninth. Again, politics was taking over. I recall Doug and I sitting and talking that night after the competition. We discussed the fact that we had skated well, yet were still behind teams that had done poorly. But I guess we were just paying our dues. It was and always will be that way in the skating world.

Isabelle

Karen Percy was the first Canadian to win a medal at the Olympics. She took the bronze for downhill skiing the day after our short program and everyone on the team was so excited. We couldn't stop talking about it.

That night, I was in the communal bathroom, brushing my teeth. A girl was standing beside me, also brushing, and she looked over and said, "Congratulations. I saw you skate and I thought you guys were very good." After asking me a few questions, she wished me luck in the long program. I prepared to leave, thinking how nice it was of this stranger to take the time to talk to me. As I was on my way out, another girl came in. I overheard her say, "Great job, Karen. Congratulations." Suddenly I realized the girl I had been speaking with was Karen Percy!

I stood outside the bathroom for a moment and thought, Oh my God. I was standing beside the athlete I had been talking about all day and I didn't even know it was her. I have always had a difficult time recognizing people because my memory is so bad. I worried about what Karen must have been thinking about me. Here I was, taking in all her praise and giving nothing back. I shook my head, went back inside and apologized to her. Karen laughed and said, "Don't worry about it. People usually don't recognize me." She was so nice about it—a true champion.

Lloyd

Isabelle and I had trouble adjusting to the altitude in Calgary and we were having a difficult time getting through the long program in our practices. Many of the Russian skaters had arrived two or three weeks early to get acclimatized but the Canadian team had not been afforded that luxury.

The venue for the long program was the Saddledome, which accommodates up to 23,000 people—a huge difference from the smaller arena where we skated the short. We went out to warm up and I noticed that Isabelle was standing at the boards, looking up at the audience. Her mouth was wide open and she had a glassy look in her eyes. I believe she was in shock over how many people were in the Saddledome and she appeared to have lost all concentration. It was obvious to me that warming up was the farthest thing from my partner's mind.

We skated around and Isabelle fell when she shouldn't have. I whispered to her, "What are you doing? Where are you?" But she paid no attention. We skated over to the boards and Josée said, "Isabelle, wake up! You are not here." We tried again and continued to fall all over the place. It was terrible. I swear that warm-up was the longest six minutes of my life. It seemed to me as if we were out there for two days. It was unbelievable. Poor Isabelle was so overwhelmed by all the people in the stadium.

After the warm-up, Josée took Isabelle aside and talked to her. Isabelle was upset, crying because we had done so poorly. I was also on edge, wondering how we were going to go out and skate. We should have been moving up in the rankings at this point but, skating like this, we didn't stand a chance.

Our turn came and I said to Isabelle, "Keep your eyes down. Just look at me . . . just look at me." But our performance was average. Mind you, it was one hundred percent better than the warm-up, and if we had had another warm-up, we would have been back on track. Our only problem was that we hadn't had much experience skating together and didn't know how to help each other through such crises. If we had been skating together longer, I might have been better able to help Isabelle cope with her nerves.

In the end, Denise and Lyndon held onto fifth, Tuffy and Doug came seventh and Isabelle and I dropped to ninth. Although we were upset for a couple of hours afterwards, we quickly let go of it and decided not to worry. We had done our best. But I think a lot of people in the skating world were saying, "See? Nationals were a fluke—Lloyd and Isabelle got lucky. Don't worry about them any more. They are going downhill from here." No one said this to us but I could sense some misgivings.

Isabelle

Practice-wise, I felt the long program was going to be all right. But when I stepped on the ice to warm up and realized there were 23,000 people in the stands, I froze. You know how some cartoon characters have a square for a body and a circle for a face? Well, that is exactly how the crowd looked to me—just a lot of squares and circles. I kept staring at all the people, and when Lloyd tried to talk to me, I couldn't answer him. I was thinking, Mom, come and take me away from here! I was totally out of it and petrified. It was the first time I had skated in front of that many people.

When the warm-up was finally over, Josée tried to calm me down. She said, "Just go out and do your own program as you do every day and don't think about the people. You will be okay." Easier said than done.

We skated the long and it wasn't our best performance but at least it was better than the warm-up. Lloyd kept trying to help me through it, saying, "I am out here with you. You are not here by yourself." I started to feel better as the program progressed and I developed more confidence with each move, but I was glad when it was over. Yet, at the same time, I wanted to do it again. One Olympics was not enough. Now that I had experienced it, I wanted to come back, but next time I would be ready for it. Lloyd and I had never been in that situation before so he didn't know how to react to me when I became that frightened.

Although we finished ninth overall, I wasn't disappointed. Of course, I would have loved to have skated better but ninth place wasn't so bad and I knew we would do better in the future.

Lloyd

Once our competitions were over, we could unwind and take in the rest of the Games. Although Isabelle and I did a lot of things together, she was only seventeen and there were places I couldn't take her, like the bars and pubs. When we were apart, we were usually with our own families and friends.

In Calgary, if you wore your Olympic jacket people would say, "Oh, you are an athlete. Come on over here and we will buy you a drink." Everybody wanted to know what sport you were in and who you were. We could leave the village with a dime in our pocket and be wined and dined all evening. People wouldn't let us buy a thing.

A favorite pastime of mine, carried over from the last Olympics, was trading possessions with other athletes. The bobsledders had taught me how to do it in Sarajevo and they had made it into an art. From the day we arrived, we started to think about what items of clothing, or whatever, we would like to get from other athletes and what we could offer in return. Some of the bobsledders brought extra clothes for just that purpose.

The best thing I traded was my marching outfit. It was a long red jacket with a detachable white fringe. I kept the fringe, which was perfect to attach my pins to. I have always collected pins from around the world. That jacket went to a Russian pairs skater for one of his ski suits that had "CCCP" printed on the back.

My most enjoyable trade was with Prince Rainier of Monaco, who was on the bobsled team. There were only four athletes from Monaco and Prince Rainier and I just happened to be about the same size. He wanted a Canadian outfit because the Olympics had been held in Canada and I thought it would be neat to have a ski outfit from an actual prince. So we traded and that ski suit is now one of my prized possessions.

The funniest trade I made was with the fellow who billeted my parents. Rick and Linda were a great couple and made us all feel comfortable in their home. They had Isabelle and me over for dinner and Rick and I had gone skiing at Lake Louise for a couple of days. At the end of the Games, some athletes were throwing a big party and, later on in the evening, we ran out of beer. Well, Rick had been admiring our ski sweaters that had the mascot of the Olympics on the front and "Olympic Team" printed on the back. He had asked me before if there was any way I could get him one. The night of the party, I remembered Rick's request and also recalled he had a couple of cases of beer at his house. I called him on the phone and said, "I'll trade you that sweater for a couple of cases of beer." Needless to say, I got my beer and Rick got his sweater.

I tried to see as many events as I could, including the bobsled run, skiing, luge, hockey and, of course, other skating. The media was focusing on the "Battle of the Brians" and everyone was speculating on who would win the competition. There was so much pressure on Brian Orser that I am not sure how he coped with it. The hierarchy of Canadian figure skating assumed he would win, and although he skated well, he took a silver to Brian Boitano's gold medal. I think it was more of a downer for everyone else than for Brian. Most people had pinned their hopes on him and in their desire for him to win had forgotten about Tracy Wilson, Rob McCall and Liz Manley.

I thought Brian had skated fantastically, with only one little slip. The powers-that-be were devastated when he didn't win and I believe it was just too much pressure to put on one kid. I don't know how he felt then but I do know that he handled himself wonderfully. I probably would have exploded if I had been in that situation.

Although I wasn't close to Liz Manley, I did know her. We had been to the 1983 Worlds together and I was happy that she was doing so well. She and the entire Canadian team were ecstatic when she won the silver and we were also pleased with Tracy and Rob's bronze in dance. Only eight medals were won by the entire Canadian Olympic team, and three of them were in figure skating.

We were allowed entry into all of these events through a lottery and I ended up with two tickets to the ladies' program and two tickets to a hockey game. Many athletes were extremely annoyed with the way the ticket system was handled. These and other events, supposedly sold out, turned out to have quite a few empty seats in the corporate sections—people weren't showing up. It bothered us that we couldn't get our parents into competitions other than our own, when all of these seats were available. Of course, I and the other skaters were at least able to gain entry without tickets. Not having a seat was fine by me.

Because I was unhappy with the ticketing arrangements, I decided to sell the tickets I had drawn. So, standing outside of the arena with my Canadian jacket on, I scalped all of them. The hockey tickets went for $500 apiece while the ladies' program brought $750 each. Maybe it was a terrible thing to do, but it was my way of protesting the system.

Isabelle

Because I was so young, I was used to having my parents at competitions, and if I wanted to go and talk to them, I could. But the Olympics was different. I couldn't see them when I wanted to and they couldn't see me. They were only allowed a one-day pass into the village for the two weeks we were there. During that visit, you were required to have a chaperon and security personnel with you, so I couldn't be with them as much as I wanted to.

But the Olympics was a great experience for me and for my parents. For once, they didn't have to take care of me; they could do what they wanted and meet other parents. That was nice for them.

I was the youngest member on the Canadian team—the baby—and people were very protective of me. Although I could leave the village whenever I wanted, I tended not to go out too much, unless there was someone with me. Often I would just go to bed early. Since I spoke mostly French and most athletes from other sports spoke English, I didn't get too involved with them and preferred to watch many events on television. Besides, it was difficult to travel to the venues, which could be miles away. It was at these Olympics that I discovered the speed skaters, and since many of them spoke French, I felt comfortable around them and grew to know them well over the next few years.

I remember meeting Gaetan Boucher, who was a superb athlete from Quebec and a hero in my province. It was his third or fourth Olympics and he was very pleasant. I couldn't believe that he took the time to be with me and showed such an interest in my career. I have a picture of him from Calgary and I will always treasure it.

One day at the village, I stood and watched in amusement for hours as other athletes, who I considered to be adults, made designs on T-shirts. It was as if they were playing and the intensity of their fun took me by surprise. Organizers had handed out white shirts to everyone, as well as a special type of glue for drawing on the T-shirts. It looked like fun, so I made a few myself. I kept two of those shirts as souvenirs: one that the other athletes helped me design and another that I designed myself. It was great, and for one afternoon I felt as if we were all the same age.

Lloyd

The closing ceremony is the time to let your hair down and enjoy yourself. Some members of the bobsled team, Doug Ladret and I had been hanging out together all day at the bars, so we were feeling pretty good by that evening.

Chris Lorri, a driver on the bobsled team, and his buddy, John Graham, used to love to do back flips. During the march into the closing ceremonies, they decided to show off their talent and I, of course, joined in. Our gymnastics made it on to national television, as well as the front page of the newspapers the next day.

We were the last athletes to our seats, which were located in an amphitheater behind the entertainment stage where k.d. lang was singing. There was also a skating show going on out in the middle of the Olympic Ice Oval. In the middle of k.d.'s song, Chris and I were suddenly overcome by the urge to help out with the tune. The next thing I knew, there were four of us on stage with k.d., dancing and belting out the song. She looked at us as if to say, What are these guys doing? But she didn't miss a beat and within seconds all of the other athletes were out of their seats and on the stage. It was a blast.

During that Olympics, I experienced so much carefree happiness. But, earlier on, something negative and totally out of my control happened that was to cost me dearly. I mention it now to show how much the media can affect anyone in the public eye.

Just prior to the Olympics, at Christmas in 1987, I had become engaged to a skater in Montreal, much to her parents' dismay. For whatever reason, they didn't like me very much and were trying to convince her not to marry me. I had invited her to the Olympics and she was to arrive just after our competition and stay for the rest of the Games. Before she arrived, I was at a skating event and my picture was taken with a group of other skaters. I happened to be sitting beside Katarina Witt and, shortly thereafter, the picture and an article appeared in the newspapers. I think the headline read, "Eisler—Rekindling an Old Flame with Katarina." The article stated that the only reason I had returned to skating was to be with Katarina again.

The whole incident was absurd but unfortunately it made the papers in Montreal the day before my fiancée was to leave for Calgary. I guess, after reading it, her parents put more pressure on her and once she arrived our relationship went downhill. She was convinced the article was true. Not long after that, I asked her to choose between her parents and me. She chose her parents.

At the time, I had no recourse to the untruths that were printed about me. Eventually, I stopped speaking to and dealing with the reporter who wrote the article but this event taught me how the media could hurt you and those close to you.

The media have such control because many people believe that everything written in newspapers is gospel. Over the years, there has been much said about me that isn't true. When a story is based on fact, I don't mind admitting the truth. But when I realized how the media could literally change a person's life, I began to hate them. I knew then that I had to do my homework and learn who the good reporters were and who the bad ones were . . . who I could talk to off the record, without worrying that they were going to misconstrue what I'd said and run to press with a story full of lies.

Sometimes, when I have been misquoted, I think I would love to stop talking to reporters altogether, but I have a habit of confronting them and they don't like it. They usually argue that I am infringing on their rights to write or say whatever they want. At that point, I tell them, "I may be infringing on your rights but if you have the right to print whatever you want, I certainly have the right to say whatever I want. I have the freedom of choice to speak my mind." I then tell them never to approach me at a press conference because I will ignore them.

These days, I seldom speak in front of large groups of reporters. In my opinion, only a handful are ethical and trustworthy. These people have my telephone number and I have theirs and we feel free to call each other when it is warranted.

There have also been books written that contain many inaccuracies. For example, Debbi Wilkes, who was once a pairs skater and is now a television commentator, recently co-authored a book on figure skating. Some of her facts were right on but, unfortunately, other information was so far out that it is difficult for a reader to know what the truth is.

I would like to stress, though, that I believe everyone has the freedom to write and say what they like. I just wish people would get their facts straight.

Isabelle

Because I had just skated at the biggest event of my life, I found the days between the Olympics and Worlds to be really difficult. It was the first time that I experienced such a letdown and I just wasn't up to going to the World Championships, which were being held in Budapest in March.

To me, Worlds seemed so small compared to the Olympics and I wasn't enthusiastic about going. I also found it hard to train. In my mind, the season was done and Josée and Eric had quite a time pushing me for two more weeks. Eric would say, "I know you don't feel like doing this but it is something you are going to have to learn. You won't always feel like doing things but that's just the way it is. This is your first Senior Worlds. Try to make it good."

His words motivated me but I still didn't feel like going. I think Lloyd was experiencing the same letdown but he had been through it before and knew how to handle it.

Because the Olympics was such a significant event for me, I have difficulty remembering much about Worlds that year. It is almost as if they didn't happen and only a couple of events stand out in my mind. The first was being at rinkside to see Kurt Browning perform the quad in competition for the first time and the second was being annoyed with Lloyd at the closing banquet.

Lloyd

Going to Budapest was great. Isabelle and I had come off a high from the Olympics and, as a result, trying to train for Worlds was awful. But we had to remember that this competition was more important than the Olympics for the placings.

I tried to let Isabelle know what to expect because I had experienced the same thing after Sarajevo, but nothing can prepare you for the downer you hit after the Olympics. You just have to try to work through it. But the time spent between the two events was incredibly tough and the weeks seemed to pass like months.

Isabelle was crying a lot because we weren't getting along with Josée and Eric, who were pushing us to work even harder than we had for the Olympics. We were just beat, physically and emotionally. I remember that we actually wondered if we should be going at all. It was that bad.

But we went to Budapest, unsure of how we would manage and we ended up skating fantastically in both the short and long. Our position from the Olympics flipped with that of Tuffy and Doug, who placed ninth behind our seventh, while Denise and Lyndon held onto fifth. We were all extremely pleased because it meant that three teams could represent Canada in Paris at the 1989 Worlds.

Budapest is very beautiful and is actually two cities—Buda and Pest, which are situated on either side of the Danube. On the day of the closing banquet, some friends and I decided to take in an outdoor wine festival, which was a forty-five-minute drive from the hotel. We arrived at 1:00 in the afternoon and spent a most enjoyable day, tasting the wines of the region. All of a sudden, someone noticed the time: it was 6:00 and the banquet was scheduled to begin in half an hour. We hailed a taxi and told the driver to go as fast as possible. Well, I thought then, if that cab ride didn't kill us, nothing would.

When I arrived back at my room, I quickly changed into a suit and happened to glance in the mirror. There was about five days' growth of beard on my face but there was no time to shave. Isabelle had slipped me a warning note under my door that began: "If you don't show up for this . . ." I ran downstairs and jumped into another cab that happened to pull up at the banquet hall right in front of Katarina Witt's taxi. Katarina was also late and the two of us walked into the crowded banquet hall together, by coincidence only. There must have been four hundred people there, from special guests to skating officials, and quite a few heads turned as Katarina and I made our entrance.

As I sat down at my assigned table, which also included the team leader and a judge, I tried to ignore their stares. I guess it was obvious that I had been drinking. The one person I couldn't ignore was Isabelle, who gave me the dirtiest look. All night long, rumors were flying about Katarina and me and I spent a great deal of time trying to get back in Isabelle's good graces. She was upset, not about Katarina, but about the fact that I had been drinking and was so late.

But I didn't mind. We had finished competing on Wednesday and it was now Sunday. So I showed up late: that was me and I didn't worry about it. Some officials gave me a hard time but I figured that was their problem.

Sometimes I get angry when people are critical of me for being myself, but most of the time I just say, "You've chosen to do it your way. I've chosen to do it my way." I believe that, although some decisions are obviously better than others, neither way is right or wrong. I am who I am and if people are uncomfortable with this, they can say or do whatever they like about it. But what they say is not going to change me in any respect and I will probably do the same thing they were critical of the next week.

Isabelle

I was ready for a vacation when I returned from Budapest and we took a couple of weeks off. Although it was the end of our season, we still had shows, exhibitions and carnivals to skate during the months of April and May.

The previous September, I had started college in my hometown so I had moved back in with my parents. I attended classes until December but decided to postpone the second semester until the following September since we were going to the Olympics and Worlds.

Right after Worlds, I started my weight training program at a gym in St-Jean. I rode there and back on my bike, five days a week, and spent two hours at the gym, lifting weights. There were two trainers and they were very good. They pushed me hard so I would build up my body.

It was then that I stopped taking the hormones and everything came together. I became stronger and stronger. At the beginning, I found it difficult, but as time went on I grew to love weight training. The only problem was, I was so focused on it that I was sometimes too sore to skate.

One night, early in the summer, I had been out for the evening and didn't get home until 1:00 a.m. My dad was waiting outside for me and he was very upset. I had just started dating Steve Ing, a fellow skater and Lloyd's roommate and I didn't think 1:00 a.m. was very late. After all, I was going to be eighteen in July and I was tired of being treated like a child. Dad and I had an argument; I went to bed angry and woke up still annoyed. To work out my frustration, I rode my bike to the gym as usual, trained for a couple of hours and then spent four or five hours riding my bike in the rain. I finally cooled off and went home. But the next day I showed up at the rink and couldn't skate. I got in trouble with my coaches. Then they put me on a scale and I weighed three pounds more than I had on the Friday.

Josée complained, "How could you have possibly gained three pounds in only one weekend?" I told them I had been working out so they measured my body fat, which turned out to be lower than it usually was. I had put on three pounds, but it was three pounds of muscle!

I kept up the body building until the 1989 Worlds, where I skated poorly. My body was just too exhausted from the intense exertion and I stopped weight training for about a year after that. I still like to work out at the gym but I have found a better balance and my schedule is much lighter.

Lloyd

I was glad when the season was over but I was really happy that we had finished on such a high note. We were scheduled to perform in several shows when we returned. Most of the shows were in Quebec, where we had become celebrities of a sort. Isabelle and I had been the first pairs team in Quebec history to make it to the Olympics and Worlds, and there was a lot of hype in the province, even though I was English.

Although we took a couple of weeks off, our real vacation wasn't until June, when we had the whole month to ourselves. I packed my 1982 Goldwing and traveled from Montreal to Seattle. My bike was loaded down as I set off, first stopping at Pam and John's in Toronto to spend the night. From there, I drove down through the United States and met up with every kind of weather. I ran into a tornado in Kansas and a temperature of 104°F in Missouri. As I was driving through the Rockies, it snowed. The trip was the ultimate vacation for me, providing the peace and solitude that I so often crave.

Isabelle

I hate skating in the summer. I am the kind of person who works best with a goal in mind. In the summer, I have no goal, and because competition time seems far away, I feel as if I don't have to train. Every summer, I felt that way but we still practiced five days a week for at least six or seven hours a day.

We usually started listening to music for our next season's programs in May or June and that year was no different. We made up the program between June and August and then started the run-throughs. That year our long program was skated to "Scheherazade" and our short was to "Dark Town Strutters Ball." Our main goal was to try to acquire a more mature look because the year before we had thrown everything together.

That summer, we began to train with Uschi Keszler, who had been Brian Orser's choreographer. I liked working with Uschi because she tried to get us to express our feelings by working with the brain more than the body. She would give Lloyd and I living examples, asking us to imagine that we were lost in a forest and to react to such a situation. From there, we learned to interpret our feelings through our skating. I was still very shy so she would take me off to work and I appreciated her sensitivity. She dealt with the expression of emotions rather than telling us, "Now you have to smile," or "Look sad," or "Place your arms here." Instead, she asked us how we felt. Uschi stressed that if a certain move didn't feel right, we didn't have to do it. We began to skate more naturally under Uschi's guidance and I soon experienced the sensation that I was floating as I was skating.

Lloyd

Probably the most dramatic change that took place that summer was that Uschi Keszler came to work with us. I knew of her work with Brian Orser but I didn't know her personally and, at that point, I didn't have a good feeling about her. She seemed to me to be a little bit off the wall. She was really bubbly and I thought she seemed extravagant. But the rapport between us quickly grew and we continued to work together until 1994.

We acquired Uschi because we were at the stage where we needed a full-time choreographer. We were looking for someone with creativity who could help us mature with fresh ideas. Isabelle and I were the first and, I think, only pairs team Uschi worked with and we were definitely ready for her. Technically, we could do everything. But our routines simply moved from element to element, trying to include all the requirements to prove what we could do.

We took some time that summer to attend the national team training camp. The whole skating team got together for a week and listened to motivational talks from the association. They basically told us what they expected from the skaters that year. New members, who had made the national team by qualifying at the Canadian championships, were inducted into the team and everyone received uniforms for the upcoming season.

Early in the summer, I moved to another apartment in Boucherville that I shared with Steve Ing. Although my partner and I skated long hours during the day, I still found it necessary to have a job and so I continued to work for Isabelle's dad at night. But I was now having fun skating, in contrast to all those years that I had trained so hard. I was enjoying myself. If I wanted to take a session off now and then, I would. My coaches were not happy with that, accusing me of being overconfident. But it wasn't like that at all. I trained as vigorously as I always had; I just didn't take it so seriously. Isabelle's dad started to make a few comments as well about missing practices and offered his opinion about what we should be doing or the direction we should be going in. During that time, he never said anything directly to me, though, only to Isabelle, and I would respond to Gill's concerns with a noncommittal, "Whatever . . ."

My mind was made up on how I was going to train and be coached, and because I had decided that we should all be in charge, there were constant battles with Josée and Eric. If, for example, Eric was yelling at Isabelle, I would approach them and begin to shout at Eric. "How do you like being yelled at?" I would ask.

He would get very angry at me and respond, "That is the way it is done." I would try and explain that it doesn't have to be that way. That was how I grew up training and I didn't want to go through it again. I wanted to have fun while I trained.

But I'd like to make it clear that, despite their methods, all of my coaches loved their kids. They were hard on them only because they thought it was in the students' best interests.

Obviously someone like myself could take this better than someone like Isabelle, who found herself in the center of things. She would often tell me that she hated being in the middle. I tried to make things easier for her by saying, "It's okay. You can side with them. I don't mind being by myself, standing alone, and arguing for us." This only made it more difficult for her.

In those days, I would try and teach Isabelle to stand up for what she believed in. I also assured her that she didn't have to be as obnoxious or as loud as I may be at times. I wanted her to let people know that she was capable of making her own decisions and that speaking up was her right. In the beginning, she didn't understand that but now she is actually much better than I am at letting people know how she feels. She is sensitive to others and has far more tact than I do.

Isabelle

I was often placed between Lloyd and my coaches during arguments and at times it really bothered me. But we were slowly learning that if Josée or Eric wanted something, it would be better to go through me. Lloyd and I had a good relationship and it was easy for me to talk to him. I was able to ask for or tell him things in a way that wouldn't upset him. Although I always seemed to be in tears about one thing or another, I got along well with both my coaches and with Lloyd. I just hated this friction between them.

Lloyd

During the summer of 1988, we developed our first signature move, which has since been named the "Brasseur-Eisler" star lift. Although there was already an element called the star lift, ours is performed differently: I lift Isabelle from the ground with only one hand, up into the star position.

It is a very difficult lift, one of the most difficult in the world, I believe. The boy has to have a lot of strength to complete it while the girl has to have leg and upper body strength to hold the position. She can't be like Jell-O or the boy won't be able to lift her.

We invented this move when Isabelle was much lighter and

continued to perform and develop it throughout our career. At the time, no one else was doing it, or even trying it, and we thought it would be fun to include in our competitions. It was then that we realized we might be able to develop other new lifts. Some people have since attempted the "Brasseur-Eisler" star lift but only a few have been successful. It is just too difficult a lift.

Isabelle

The opening competition of the season was to be Skate Canada at Thunder Bay. It was the first time that our new programs would be viewed by international judges and that we would compete against people who had been at Worlds the year before. Two of the teams we were to compete against had placed third and fourth at Worlds.

We turned in outstanding performances for both the short and long programs and won the competition. People loved our new look and our star lift. Everyone commented as well on the height of our triple and double twists. Lloyd and I believed that our new-found maturity was showing through as well in the way we were now interpreting the music.

We skated a fun number for the exhibition, choreographed by John Thomas, and since it was Halloween, we decided to adapt our costumes for a party we were to attend that night. We dressed identically, wearing white T-shirts. Mine had "Betty" printed on the back and Lloyd's read "Al." We wore three-quarter-length trousers, suspenders and baseball hats, with the brim off to one side and our eyes and teeth were blackened. We thoroughly enjoyed ourselves that night. Of course, coming first at the competition didn't dampen our festive mood.

Lloyd

It was only October and having placed first at Skate Canada, the pressure was already on us for the next Worlds. We skated well and people were now telling us what to do to stay on top. But Isabelle and I were just having fun. Of course, we were excited. It was the first Skate Canada that I had ever won and Isabelle's first and my second win at an international competition.

After the competition, we performed a show number called "Betty and Al" for the exhibition, to music by Paul Simon. This was our first exhibition number that had more flair than usual and that we had made up for sheer entertainment. Usually, skaters perform part of their competition number for the exhibition. Our number went over so well that we started to think, This may be our niche.

Because of our win at Skate Canada, Isabelle and I began the skating year feeling higher than you can imagine. Little did we know that the 1989 season was to be the lowest point in our career.

That December, we went with Uschi to Broadmoor, Colorado, to perform a "Symphony on Ice" show. It was held outdoors and the scenery was breathtakingly beautiful. Isabelle and I had been spending more and more time together and were getting along really well. We took long walks around the lake and visited the zoo. I was thoroughly enjoying Isabelle's company and decided to send her a dozen roses. Although nothing was said, I realized that our relationship was changing and suddenly I was looking at my partner through new eyes.

Isabelle

I had stopped dating Steve in early December. Lloyd and I were traveling a lot together as usual but things seemed to be changing between us. At the Olympics and Worlds, although Lloyd tended to look after me, he had his friends and I had mine, so we were usually doing our own thing. After Steve and I broke up, I began to spend more time with Lloyd, pursuing activities outside of skating.

Just before Christmas we went to Colorado, where the whole atmosphere was very romantic with the outdoor lake and the lights. I felt very close to Lloyd by that point and our relationship seemed to take on a new meaning. Where this would lead to, I had no idea. I only knew that we were enjoying all of the time we spent together and I couldn't wait to discover what the new year would bring.

CHAPTER FIVE

Decisions

Isabelle

A s Lloyd and I counted down the seconds to January 1, 1989, I sensed our relationship had taken on new depth and meaning. We had been skating partners for two years and close friends for the last several months. Now, there was more.

We decided to keep these feelings secret for a while. After all, people were just getting used to the fact that we were committed as partners on the ice. At this stage, there was no point in letting everyone know that our relationship now extended beyond the arena.

I was also wary of what my dad's reaction would be. He had just been through open-heart surgery to correct a valve. Although he was out of the hospital, he still wasn't working and was trying to change his lifestyle to keep it as stress-free as possible. So I felt it was best to see where Lloyd and I were going before rocking an already shaky boat.

Nationals were to be held in Chicoutimi, Quebec, in February and I was looking forward to competing in my home province. It was during a practice for this championship that I first experienced pain in my ribs while doing the triple lateral twist, which we had just invented. People were performing doubles but no one had attempted a triple, and at the time of this writing no one else has yet performed it. In this element, I go up about 12 to 15 feet in the air in the star position and turn three times laterally, then come down feet first. Lloyd catches me and places me on the ice. This difficult element appeared to be bruising my ribs, and resulted in much discomfort for me.

During this time, my father decided that my competitions were causing too much worry for him. He had always been heavily involved in my skating and would become very nervous for me. If I made a mistake, he would just get too upset. Dad finally came to the conclusion that seeing me compete wasn't good for his health and chose to no longer attend my competitions. What could I say? I had to respect his decision. I loved having my parents at the competitions but more than anything I just wanted my dad to get better.

Lloyd

I asked Isabelle out to dinner on New Year's Eve. We went to a restaurant in Montreal that has since become one of our favorites and had a great time. From that night on, we began to see each other more outside the rink and eased into a dating situation. We did all the things people do when they go out together and before long I was spending more time with than without Isabelle.

At the beginning, we elected not to tell anyone. Friends and other skaters would ask if we were dating but we denied it for the first few months, wanting to keep our personal lives to ourselves. We knew what some people would say and Isabelle was very worried about how her family would react, especially her father.

Although she never said anything, I think Josée picked up on our relationship right away. She and Isabelle were always very close and Josée had an uncanny knack of knowing what was happening with Isabelle.

Because my partner and I were spending more time together away from skating, we began to open up to one another in a way we hadn't before. The side of our personalities that was rarely revealed while we skated began to emerge and we were better able to tune in to each other's emotions. I think that connection began to express itself on the ice and, in the beginning, it definitely enhanced our skating.

As we prepared for the 1989 Canadian championships, we made some changes in our long program. Although it had worked well for us the previous fall, we threw in some elements to help build our confidence level. Isabelle and I needed all the assurance we could get, since we would be competing against everyone who had beaten us at Worlds the year before.

Absolutely no one expected us to win at this Nationals, with Lyndon and his new partner, Cindy Landry, being favored to take the top prize. After the short program, though, Isabelle and I were in second place, much to the excitement of the audience, who were obviously rooting for the Quebec-based team. We were behind Cindy and Lyndon and ahead of Tuffy and Doug.

The night of the long program saw us skate very well and when the marks were tallied, we had won! We were national champions for the first time together and we couldn't believe it. Our win surprised many people, including Cindy and Lyndon, as well as Isabelle and me. It was a very emotional time for me because the win marked my return to the top of my field in Canada. I had won the championship in 1984 and it had taken me five years to reclaim the title. It was a long, hard struggle but I was finally back at the pinnacle of my game and was determined we were going to stay there.

Isabelle

I had never won a National championship before, and when we realized that we had come first, it was one of the most exciting moments of my life. We were the best in our sport in Canada and a dream of mine had finally come true. Unfortunately, it was also a sad time for me. Not having my parents there left me with the feeling that the event wasn't complete.

They still didn't know about Lloyd and me, and although I felt close to them, I no longer lived with them. At the end of 1988, I had leased an apartment in Boucherville, thinking it was time to be on my own. My parents and I discussed it, and although they were reluctant, they weren't opposed to it either. I was attending college and skating in Boucherville and they realized it was best for me to live there, but I promised them I would return home as often as I could. Dad was worried about me driving on the icy roads in winter, though: to save me the trip, he would come to Boucherville at least a couple of times a week.

I lived in that apartment for five years and I loved it. It was a tiny place but I never lacked for roommates. My door was open to anybody who needed somewhere to stay, whether it was for one month or a year.

Lloyd

The 1989 Worlds were in Paris and people were expecting big things from Isabelle and me. That was the first year pairs skaters were allowed to do a double Axel in the short program. This was tough for us because Isabelle's double Axel was not consistent; it was the weak link in our program. We hadn't performed it at Nationals, where we had opted for the less difficult double Lutz, but we wanted to perform it at Worlds.

Just before we left, the CFSA informed us that Josée wouldn't be able to attend the competition as our coach. We were stunned. Not having our coach with us was unthinkable. Apparently, CFSA rules stated that a coach had to have certain levels of certification in Canada to go to Worlds. At that time, Josée didn't have all her levels and she wasn't considered to be an accredited coach. They told us to take Eric instead, even though we explained that Josée always accompanied us to competitions. This was a real kick in the teeth because we were simply trying to get ahead and we felt as if the CFSA was not behind us. I recall making some pretty harsh accusations against them at the time. I believed they were favoring Mr. Leitch's teams because there was more communication with him than there was with Josée and Eric, who were in Quebec. Mr. Leitch was and continues to be very involved with the CFSA.

We left for Worlds amid all this turmoil and with Eric acting as our head coach. Josée came but was not allowed to speak to Isabelle or me during practices. They wouldn't let her down at ice level: she had to sit in the stands. This wasn't good for Isabelle as she needed Josée's light-hearted approach to feel good about competing. The whole thing really ticked me off and was extremely disheartening for both of us.

I also had a virus to contend with in Paris, and other than going to practice, I was in bed for three days prior to the competition. I couldn't stomach any food and my temperature soared to 103°F. On the day of the short program, I managed to eat a banana, just to get some potassium into my system. Isabelle helped me as much as she could, doing all the work that I would normally do, such as getting our costumes ready.

Since we had nothing to lose, we decided to go for the double Axel in the short program. Unfortunately, Isabelle missed hers and we placed eighth out of eleven contenders. Cindy and Lyndon elected to do a double Lutz, skated cleanly and placed second.

We didn't skate much better in the long and ended up finishing seventh. I remember coming off the ice and feeling really down. I was also very angry about our performance. Because I had been ill, I hadn't performed to the best of my ability and Isabelle had also missed some of her jumps. We obviously had our reasons for skating poorly but none of them seemed to justify the outcome. Cindy and Lyndon took the silver. I couldn't help but think, that since we had just beaten them at Nationals, that spot could and should have been ours. But it wasn't meant to be.

We had come seventh for two years in a row, and although there was much improvement, we had made no progress in the placings. Isabelle and I had just failed to put it all together. We had a great autumn, a fantastic Nationals and ended on a sour, sour note. And that is what everyone, including ourselves, remembered about the 1989 season.

Isabelle

Coming seventh at Worlds wasn't so bad. What was upsetting was that we had skated so poorly. Many of the top skaters from the year before had retired or moved on to become professionals, and people were looking at us to move up to that level. I became very nervous with all the attention and missed my jumps. Every time Lloyd would let go of me, I would fall. The competition was a huge disappointment.

Lloyd wasn't really angry with me. I was more upset with myself and wondered if I wanted to continue skating. I just didn't know if I could do it anymore. As soon as Worlds were over I returned home, and the next morning I was on the first flight to Florida, where my parents were vacationing. I just needed to be with people who loved me for myself and not for my career. Intending on spending only a weekend with them, I wound up staying for three weeks. We canceled all our shows, which we had never done before or since, and I questioned whether I wanted to stay in the sport.

Lloyd joined me in Florida and the two of us talked everything out with my mom and dad. We had recently broken the news to them about our relationship. Although they weren't enthusiastic in the beginning because they worried about the age difference, they soon became accustomed to us being a couple.

With a little bit of a vacation and a lot of communication, we realized what skating meant to us and reluctantly decided to continue. But, to do that, we had to make some changes.

The first thing to go was the dramatic type of program we had done the previous season. We had skated the "Scheherazade" number well a few times but it really wasn't us, so we opted to return to our lively style and just skate. That summer, we trained heavily and spent much of our time with Dr. Peter Jensen, who helped us figure out where we were going and how to get there. He also helped me with psychological training on my double Axel. In late August, we headed down to the States to develop our programs with Uschi. There, we gained a different perspective, and when we came back we were ready to skate.

By this time, Josée and Eric knew about my off-ice relationship with Lloyd but they never offered any advice one way or the other. They are the type of people who believe it's best to "live and let live."

As my involvement with Lloyd continued to develop, it seemed that we were bickering more during our skating sessions. The more familiar we became with each other, the more we felt we had the right to speak up and say what was on our minds. That often led to loud arguments, which sounded awful at the time but which, in a way, were good for us. They helped to get our frustrations out of our systems right away. Some days, we would lose a whole session, yelling at each other and saying what we really thought. But the next day we would skate well because we had cleared the air of tension. Our arguments were centered on skating. Away from the arena, Lloyd and I got along very well and rarely fought.

Lloyd

After Worlds, Isabelle and I seriously considered quitting skating. We took a vacation and talked everything through. Although we decided to give it another try, our minds were still focused on the negative aspects. We thought that the year had been too tough and that maybe we should just throw in the towel. Maybe all of those doubters had been right. Maybe we had just been lucky when we won Nationals. Maybe it wasn't going to work after all. Maybe, maybe, maybe . . . Those thoughts plagued us from March to August.

It was a long summer with lots of fighting. Every time a session didn't go well, one of us would say, "Hey, let's just quit," and we constantly debated the issue. Should we quit? Should we not quit? We always seemed to be in the middle of an argument about it with either each other or Josée and Eric. This got us nowhere and finally we realized we had to get away from our environment. We had never been apart from Josée and Eric but one day Isabelle and I looked at each other and said, "Let's leave. Let's just go somewhere." So we went to Delaware to work with Uschi. I knew we needed the change and I believed that a different atmosphere could help. I also thought, If this doesn't work, our skating will be over.

While in Delaware, we also trained with Ron Luddington and Bob Young. Mr. Luddington was the head coach at the center. I had known and liked him for a number of years while I had been with Mr. Leitch. It wasn't until Isabelle and I returned in September that we at last saw improvement in our skating. It had been an awful spring and a terrible summer; nothing had been accomplished. But, in two short weeks, we had made up our minds to stick with it and get on with our careers.

Our programs for the 1990 season were a lot more dynamic than the previous year's numbers. The short program, set to circus music, was especially fun. The test for the programs was our first fall competition, Skate Electric in England. We had been training very well and felt much better about our future.

I had been to this particular competition in 1981, where my partner and I had won, and I knew all about the rink. Although Isabelle and I had a couple of bad practices, we skated our best during the competition and won. But the real confidence booster for us was that Isabelle landed the double Axel during both programs. She had missed it back in March at Worlds, when it had counted so much, and now in the first competition of the year, she couldn't have performed it better.

In those days, skaters could pick which competitions they wanted to participate in and Isabelle had decided to return to Paris. She declared, "I want to go and skate at that rink as I should have skated at Worlds." So off to Paris we went, determined to win the *Trophée Lalique* and beat the rink that had put our career in so much jeopardy. Although we skated very well and Isabelle again landed the double Axel, we came second. But we weren't at all disappointed. We were happy with how we had skated and, in our minds, had overcome the rink that had given us so much trouble.

Isabelle and I came home and won the Divisionals. We weren't required to participate but we really wanted to. Everyone loved the new programs and we felt very prepared for the 1990 Canadian championships.

Isabelle

We thought we were ready for Nationals in Sudbury and skated a good first program. In fact, we were the only team to skate the double Axel clean. But, for whatever reasons, Lloyd and I were sitting in the second position after the short program. Then came the long and we skated poorly. We barely made it on to the world team as we came third by the score of only one judge. One judge—and we wouldn't have made it.

Lloyd

Cindy and Lyndon did a double Lutz in their short program and we performed a double Axel. They missed their jump and still beat us. We were furious and we looked at each other and asked, "What is the deal here?" Isabelle and I had done exactly what we were supposed to do and yet we came second. The politics of Nationals was becoming a real joke.

Because the CFSA was located in Ontario and we were a Quebec-based team, we believed we were getting the brunt of the association's not wanting to have anything to do with our province. It was disheartening because, again, we didn't feel they were supporting us as much as we would have liked. But Josée maintained, "Don't worry about them. We are doing it for us."

We skated the long and I don't know what happened. Isabelle just fell apart and we skated poorly. We fell two or three times and dropped to third. Cindy and Lyndon came first and Tuffy and Doug second. Out of the nine judges, five of them awarded us third place and four gave us fourth. By one judge's score, we had made Worlds, which were going to be held in Halifax. Isabelle and I had no idea how close the score was until the night of the closing banquet, when we received the protocol that lists the ordinals and marks. We had actually made it by *only one point*. Imagine if we had missed Worlds in our own country! Until that night, we had no idea how lucky we were to come third.

Isabelle

When we arrived home, Josée and Eric informed us they hadn't been too impressed with our performance at Nationals. The next day, we were training for Worlds and practicing the long program. At one point, Lloyd stopped. When Eric saw this, he said, "From now on, you must move forward. You cannot stop in the middle of a program. I want you to do every single element."

Lloyd started to disagree with him quite loudly and Eric remarked, "If you want to take that attitude, fine. We are not going to be at Worlds to see you skate the way you just did at Nationals." Lloyd and Eric argued a little more and then Eric and Josée simply stopped coaching us.

For the next two weeks, Lloyd and I trained very hard by ourselves. We decided to concentrate solely on our skating and let nothing interfere with it. During that time of intensive training, we were both so strained and tired that we didn't have the energy to do anything else, even fight. Extra hours of ice time were booked and Lloyd and I practiced three programs a day. Sometimes it would be two long and one short or two short and one long but we made sure we performed one perfectly every day.

I went to see my Dad a few days before leaving for Worlds. He and my mom hadn't been to any of my competitions since his heart surgery and I desperately missed having my parents with me at these important moments in my life. I said, "Dad, I really want you at my competitions. I can't skate when you aren't there. You have changed so much and are not controlling my life anymore. I need you." But he resisted.

My brother decided that someone from the family should be at Worlds and bought tickets to attend the competition. This made me feel better but I still hoped that my dad would change his mind.

Two days before I left for Halifax, I was staying at our house in St-Jean. My parents were out for the evening but I couldn't sleep and waited for their return. When they arrived home, my dad was surprised to see that I was still awake. He asked, "What are you doing? You are leaving in two days. Shouldn't you be in bed?"

I started to cry and through my sobs whispered, "Dad, do you not want to come to my competition because last year at Worlds I fell down so much? Are you ashamed because I can't stay on my feet?"

He didn't take what I had said too well, and in the morning I left for Boucherville. That day he called me and asked, "Do you think you can find your mother and me two tickets for Halifax?" Needless to say, I was overjoyed.

Lloyd

In 1990, between the Nationals and Worlds, I was not getting along with Josée and Eric. I got into a huge fight with Eric, who had told us to repeat the long program we had been working on. He demanded, "Do it again."

"No," I answered. "We tried it. It wasn't that good and we will do it again tomorrow."

"Fine," he replied. "Josée and I will not coach you until you do what we tell you to do."

So I said, "Good. Leave. I don't need you." Isabelle began to cry. We sat down together and I tried to comfort her. We talked and agreed to practice on our own, and for the next two weeks we trained harder than if our coaches had been there. We took extra ice time and did more run-throughs than usual, but not all in the same session. Gradually, our skating improved as we worked on each of the elements. It was hard on Isabelle, though, and periodically she would say, "I hate not having my coach here."

Three days before we left for Worlds, Josée came down to the ice. She commented on how well we were doing and asked if there was anything she could help us with. Isabelle and I had already decided not to hold a grudge and Josée began to work with us again. But Eric was still upset and chose not to join us at that time.

In retrospect, I think they made the right decision to leave us alone, even though it had stemmed from an argument. It wasn't that I thought I could coach myself. I believe that no matter how talented you are, you can't objectively see yourself perform. No matter how good it feels, you need feedback from another party. In my opinion, athletes who believe they can coach themselves are crazy. But being on our own for those two weeks certainly forced us to get our act together.

Isabelle

Upon our arrival in Halifax, our confidence level really began to escalate, especially since Josée was with us. She had received her coaching accreditation and was once again allowed to attend Worlds.

We were the third-last team to skate in the short program and when we stepped onto the ice, the crowd went wild with enthusiasm, as they had with all the Canadian skaters. We skated well but, just as importantly, I landed the double Axel. I was so elated that I couldn't sleep that night.

For the long program, we were competing against some of the top people who were at the Olympics in 1988. We skated amazingly, and for the last thirty seconds of our number, the audience took to their feet. The feeling I had was beyond description. Lloyd and I were so excited with the way we skated that we could have placed fourth and still have been happy. But we took the silver behind Gordeeva and Grinkov's gold and ahead of Dmitriev and Mishkutenok's bronze.

When we stood on the podium and received our medals, I couldn't believe it was happening. What topped it off to make it a perfect memory was knowing that all of the people who were important to me were there to share in my moment of joy.

Lloyd

Only Josée went with us to Halifax. Since Eric and I still weren't speaking, Josée felt he should stay home. Isabelle and I were feeling good, though. Because we had gotten used to doing complete run-throughs, we did the same during practices and skated clean most of the time.

The short program saw Isabelle and I following the other Canadians. Tuffy and Doug had skated well, whereas Cindy and Lyndon had not. Lyndon missed his double Lutz. This was rare for him: Lyndon was one of the most consistent skaters I knew.

Just before our names were called to perform, Josée took us to one side and said, "You came seventh last year and seventh the year before. You have nothing to lose. If you don't do well, we will quit and a decision will have been made. You have worked hard so just go out and enjoy the program."

We started off with a big double twist and received thunderous applause from an appreciative home crowd. Coming up to the double Axel, we talked to each other using key words. Isabelle did the jump as if she had never missed it and the audience was ecstatic. The rest of the program ran smoothly, and when we finished, Isabelle and I stood and hugged each other for what seemed like minutes but in reality was only seconds. We skated off the ice and Josée, who had asked Ron Luddington to stand beside her during the program because she was so nervous, was jumping up and down with excitement. I can't recall our marks but when we found out we were fourth, behind the Russian teams, we couldn't believe it. We had expected fifth or even sixth place.

The next day during practice, we couldn't land a single jump. I am not sure if it was the excitement from the night before. Isabelle hadn't slept well and I was very anxious to perform that night. We came off the ice, arguing with each other, and then I began to take out my frustrations on Josée. She looked at me and calmly said, "I am leaving. Goodbye," and walked away in the middle of the practice. Isabelle and I went back on the ice and continued to fall all over the place.

By the end of the session, we had talked our way back to civility with each other and went to look for Josée. When we caught up with her, the three of us spoke for over an hour and our coach reminded us that we had lost our perspective as to why we were skating and what our job was. Josée put our reasons for being there back in our heads and our hearts.

Isabelle and I were last to skate for the long, which put additional pressure on us. Before warm-up, I remember feeling a sense of wonder that we were in the top group, with Gordeeva and Grinkov, who had won the Olympics in 1988 and Worlds in 1989. This was to be their last competition before retiring from the amateur level for the first time.

Everyone else skated and didn't perform as well as expected, especially Gordeeva and Grinkov, who missed some things, which was unusual for them. When it was our turn, we stepped onto the ice, looked at each other and said, "Let's go out and have fun." And that is just what we did, skating flawlessly in the process.

In the middle, there was a pause in the program and we were standing quite close to the boards and the television announcers. Tracy Wilson was sitting right there and, as we stopped, I was so relaxed that I looked at Tracy and the others and said, "This one is for you guys," meaning the program. I knew they were hoping Isabelle and I would do well. We finished the program, but for the last thirty or forty seconds we couldn't hear the music. The crowd were on their feet, clapping long before the end. The last move in the program was our triple lateral twist, but by then we were so tired and excited that I didn't see the sense in attempting it, so I said to Isabelle, "Just do a double." As the number closed, we stood there with huge grins on our faces, positive we had done the best job we could.

Skating over to the boards, we met up with a tearful Josée and others who kept repeating, "You two are going to win. You and Isabelle deserve the win." When the scores were finally tallied, though, we placed second but were elated with the realization. The jubilation that surrounded us was overwhelming. Isabelle and I couldn't believe we had taken the silver. Our parents, who were celebrating with us, were as shocked and excited as we were.

The outcome of that competition marked the beginning of our pressure-filled career. From then on, people expected us to always do that well. But that night Isabelle and I weren't thinking beyond the moment: we simply savored the taste of winning silver at the Worlds.

Isabelle

Because we had placed second, Lloyd and I were invited on the ISU tour throughout the United States. Since the Worlds had been held in North America, the tour was combined with the Tom Collins Tour of Olympic and World Figure Skating Champions, which also usually took place at this time.

I had no idea what was involved, having never been on a tour before, but I had such a fun time. We visited many cities and states and performed in about fifteen shows in the three weeks we were away. There was also plenty of time in between engagements for sightseeing and shopping. It was on this tour that I became good friends with Kristi Yamaguchi and Mark Mitchell. The only drawback was, because I was underage, I couldn't go to bars with Lloyd at night. So he would be off somewhere with his friends and I would be back at the hotel with mine.

Lloyd

On the last night of Worlds, Tom Collins met with us and invited Isabelle and me to go on his tour, which was held in conjunction with the ISU tour. The invitation came so late that I was beginning to wonder if we would be asked at all. There had been a rumor that the CFSA had advised Tom not to take us because I was a rebel and would cause problems on his tour.

When I heard this rumor, I mentioned it to Josée, who told me not to worry about it. "If they don't take you, we will go home and start working toward next year," she said. I was at the stage, though, where I would have liked to earn some money from my skating. Not only that, I was getting fed up with the CFSA's politics.

Every year after Worlds, the winners of the national championships in all the categories of skating were invited by Tom Collins to tour the United States with his show. Tommy and his brothers used to be an act in "Holiday on Ice." He eventually organized his own tour and has been doing it for the past fifteen years. What started out as a small show is now considered to be the "Cadillac of Tours" by skaters. Tommy, who is a great guy, provides the best of everything for us. Now, both amateurs and professionals join his tour, but back in 1990 it was strictly amateur and provided a way for us to earn some money to help fund our careers.

When Tuffy and Doug won Nationals in 1988, they were invited on the tour. When Isabelle and I won in 1989 but did poorly at the Worlds, we were bypassed and Tom took Cindy and Lyndon, who had come second at Worlds. Now, we were second at Worlds and Cindy and Lyndon were ninth, although they had come first at Nationals. So I waited to see who the CFSA was going to recommend to Tommy to invite, as that was usually the procedure.

Tom finally came to me and said, "I have been told by several of the powers-that-be that maybe I shouldn't take you and Isabelle on my tour because you are going to cause problems."

His comments didn't surprise me. I told him, "I'm not going to pretend that I am a perfect little boy and that I don't say or do whatever I want to, but when it comes to skating and doing what I am supposed to do, I am always one hundred percent there."

Tommy grinned and said, "Well, we are inviting you on the tour and think you will do very well." He had made up his own mind and I respected him for that.

Shortly after, I discovered that Cindy and Lyndon were also invited and I blew my stack at the association. I said in disbelief, "Tuffy and Doug won two years ago and you recommended them. We won last year and you bypassed us. This year, because they are national champions, you are inviting them?" I was fuming but I also realized the circumstances of the decision. I knew the association and Mr. Leitch were close and that Josée and Eric were not quite as politically associated. There wasn't much I could do, so I let it go.

We didn't have an agent at the time, although I was hoping someone would take us on. But it seemed that no one wanted us or was even interested. I tried to shop ourselves around but I couldn't get any takers. The tour was our first opportunity to make some money, and since we were without an agent, Josée looked after things for us.

For the shows, we chose "Dark Town Strutters Ball" and "Salsa." Originally, we performed the more serious program first and then "Salsa" as an encore. For some reason, our programs weren't received as well as they should have been and the organizers asked us to do only one number instead of two. We were opposed to this idea. Everyone else who was second in the world had two numbers and we weren't about to give up one of ours. Tommy and I discussed the matter and he suggested switching the order of the programs. We agreed and they went over one hundred percent better with the audience. I think it was because "Salsa" was trick oriented. We were beginning to acquire that flair for drama, and when the crowd saw us do that number, they became really interested in our skating.

We loved the tour life . . . absolutely loved it. We had a great time, made a lot of friends and saw everything there was to see. I can recall one incident during that particular tour: we didn't think anything of it then but laugh about it now.

Martin Smith, who was Canadian dance champion, Kurt Browning, Todd Eldredge and I were in a hotel room in San Francisco, playing "Bunny Ball," a game we had invented to while away the hours. It was a little like baseball, but instead of a ball we used a stuffed rabbit Kurt had received from a fan. We were twenty-eight floors up and had the window open. One of us hit the bunny right out the window—it was like a home run that went over the fence. The "ball" landed on a ledge outside and since we wanted to keep playing, we decided to retrieve it. Martin, Kurt and I hung Todd by his feet, out the window and, in the process, almost dropped him.

When we managed to pull an ashen-faced Todd back inside, he said in a small voice, "You guys almost dropped me. I could have died."

We nonchalantly answered, "Oh yeah . . . well, don't worry about it. Who's up?" We had our bunny back and just wanted to resume the game.

Isabelle

At the beginning of our relationship, I couldn't wait to spend time with Lloyd, and because we grew so close, I think it showed on the ice as our skating improved. But we were spending so many hours together that it almost became too much. Outside of the arena, our relationship was good but we were now having a hard time getting along while skating. Lloyd wanted to do things one way and I, another. Little annoyances began to irritate us and because we were so comfortable with each other, we sometimes said things that we later regretted.

Lloyd and I are obviously very different and there are many areas that we don't necessarily agree on. He is outspoken while I tend to be more withdrawn. While we were dating, if Lloyd made a comment that I didn't think was appropriate, it bothered me because I felt more responsible for him. We were a part of each other and I always felt as if I had to fix whatever was broken. If we had been just skating partners, those things probably wouldn't have upset me the same way.

At the beginning of the summer, we talked and came to the realization that if we were going to continue to see each other, we would probably have to stop skating. Neither of us wanted that to happen. Our careers were too important to us. So, after much thought, we decided to go our separate ways as far as our personal lives were concerned. We agreed that if we were meant to be together, then it would happen. But, in the meantime, we must sacrifice our love to keep skating together.

After this decision was made, I have to admit I had a hard time. It was so difficult to work with each other every day and I suppose it took me at least a year to really accept it. Sometimes I would see Lloyd and wonder, Is this really over?

For the first six or seven months, we spent our free time with our own friends instead of together or with mutual friends. We found it easier that way. When Lloyd began to date other people, I didn't always like it and I think it was the same with him. But we both respected our decision and, in time, began to get along better. Lloyd and I were still friends throughout this period but it took us a while before we were able to speak freely with each other again, especially about other people we were dating. Our relationship had been too serious to get over quickly. It was going to take time.

Lloyd

Isabelle and I had gone out for a while and, I think, in the beginning it was needed to bring us closer. Once we started to climb to higher levels in skating, the pressure was on and suddenly we found that we were arguing on the ice about something that happened yesterday or something that was going on in our personal lives.

I was more worried about losing Isabelle's friendship, trust and respect than I was concerned about having a girlfriend. I thought long and hard about it and came to the conclusion that there was no way around the problem. Although it was going to be a very tough thing to do, our dating would have to end.

After a lot of discussion, Isabelle and I broke up that summer. It was extremely difficult for both of us and we were both hurting. There always seemed to be a cutting remark flung from one of us to the other and I recall having big fights both on and off the ice. The arguments, which had nothing to do with skating, were just a result of trying to deal with a painful situation.

Isabelle

By the time we got back on the ice, we were way behind the other senior pairs skaters in our school. We had returned from the tour in the middle of May and wanted to take some time off. Josée preferred to start training immediately but we were adamant about taking a vacation.

Everyone else had picked their music and were halfway through their programs, while Lloyd and I were just trying to skate around the ice. We were also in the midst of trying to cope with our breakup and it was a very emotional time for us both.

Lloyd

That summer, Isabelle and I began to set our own schedule. We had taken a month off after the tour. I had just purchased and moved into my condominium and was excited about having a place of my own.

We showed up about two weeks late for summer school and changed the way we viewed our training. Gradually, we learned how to train through the year to be good from January through March, as opposed to being at our best in the autumn to make it to Worlds. We went on the assumption that we would make it to Worlds and that is where we wanted to be at our peak.

It was a difficult summer, to say the least. Not only were we dealing with our personal problems but Isabelle was very worried that we were not going to be ready for the season. She was concerned that the other teams in our school, who had now turned senior and would be competing against us, were much further ahead. She would watch them and say, "Look. They are better than we are."

Once again, we headed down to the States to work with Ron, Bob and Uschi, who choreographed the new numbers. Our short program was set to Charleston music, complete with the 1920s style of costume. The long was also very upbeat. It was a powerful number with a slow part in the middle and a lot of high-speed moves.

That fall, we competed in Skate Canada, held in Lethbridge, Alberta. Our new numbers went over well and we won the competition. From there, we went to Japan for the NHK Trophy and came second because we missed the double Axel in the short program. I was a little discouraged. It felt like . . . Oh no, here we go again.

Isabelle

One night in December, I received a phone call from Lloyd. He said, "I have a bit of a problem. I can't move." He went on to tell me that he had injured his knee while playing hockey but promised he would have it looked at right away. The next time I heard from Lloyd, he was freaking out. He was in Toronto, where his doctor had told him he required immediate surgery.

I was upset, obviously, because my partner was in pain but also because we had a show to do in a few days. We just couldn't pull out because all the big names had already withdrawn and Lloyd and I felt obligated to perform. I was also worried how his injury might affect our career. He came home with a huge brace on his leg, which he couldn't even put weight on. But Lloyd was determined to skate that weekend. I have to tell you, the whole thing was really scary.

Lloyd

December 12, 1990, is forever etched in my mind. It was on that date that I came very close to losing my career. I had been playing hockey in the senior league, which I had done twice a week for a number of years. I was on a break-away, tried to deke the goalie and got my skate edge caught—I did score, though. Heading straight for the net's post, I managed to get my body out of the way but my left knee hit the post dead-on and the momentum flung me around.

I was lying behind the net and, for a moment, seriously thought my leg was left in front of it. Looking down, I was grateful to see my limb still with me. But the pain was tremendous. I couldn't get up on my own. With the help of my teammates, I slowly made it over to the bench.

We were winning the game and I didn't want to take my pads

off, just in case I would be able to play again, so I iced my knee through the pads. I thought maybe it was just a bad bruise, so throughout a couple of shifts, I bent and stretched it and then went back on the ice. I completed two more shifts, scored another goal and was happy that we won the game.

When I finally took off my equipment, my knee had swollen to the size of a football and, after I showered and dressed, I was barely able to walk. Once at home, the first person I telephoned was Isabelle, who advised me to get it checked out right away. I figured it was serious enough to warrant a call to my doctor in Toronto, who told me I had better see him as soon as possible.

I booked a flight that evening and went directly to the hospital, where I met with Dr. Brock. After he and three other orthopedic surgeons checked it out, they told me I needed surgery right away. They proclaimed, "You won't be doing Nationals but if we can get you a buy, you just may be ready for Worlds."

"But I have a show to do on Sunday," I replied. It was a benefit in Montreal for the Quebec Figure Skating Federation, and because another couple had canceled, Isabelle and I were the headliners. The doctors just looked at me and laughed. I said, "No, you don't understand. I *must* do Nationals come February and I would also like to skate on Sunday. As far as surgery goes," I continued, "that will have to wait until June. Now, what can I do to make this possible?"

After telling me I was crazy and couldn't possibly last until June, Dr. Brock suggested a full leg brace that would give me some stability. It was known as a "Generation Two." But he warned me that it was not a cure, simply an aid. The doctors then said that I had only a twenty-five percent chance of being ready for Nationals, a fifty percent chance of being able to skate at Worlds and absolutely no way I would be able to perform on Sunday.

I slept at Dr. Brock's house that night and in the morning we were off to Sport Mate, which makes the special brace. A cast was formed of my leg and the brace was made that day. Usually, this procedure would take a couple of weeks.

I was back home by Saturday and on the ice. But what a joke. I

(left) Tom Collins Tour, Albany 1992: this is Isabelle's most precious picture of her dad—the last photograph of the two of them taken before he died.

(below) Phoenix, Arizona, during a day off on the 1992 Tom Colins Tour: playing in the pool are Isabelle, Lloyd and Kristi Yamaguchi.

(above left) Lloyd, his mother Bev, his younger sister Mary Jane, Lloyd Sr. at Mary Jane's University of Tennesee graduation in 1993. (above right) Lloyd and his older sister, Marie Gardner, in Arlington, Washington on horseback.

(above left) Lloyd Sr., Isabelle, Claudette, and Lloyd at 1993 World's, after the short program. (above right) 1993 World's, at end of the long program.

Isabelle and roomie Nancy Kerrigan in 1993, at the Hotel
Laguna Nagual Californie, on the last day of the tour.

European tour in 1993, when Isabelle hit Lloyd in the eye.

1994 Opening Ceremonies in Lillehammer. The "girls" from left to right: Josée Chouinard, Susan Humphreys, Kristy Sargeant, Isabelle, Jamie Salé and Josée Picard.

Isabelle and Lloyd at the Closing Ceremonies at the 1994 Olympics in Lillehammer.

(above left) Isabelle and her mother, Claudette, at the 1994 CFSA Volunteer Achievement award. (above right) Isabelle and Julie Marcotte, choreographer and best friend.

Lloyd and Isabelle with close friends Pamela and John Boniferro.

(above left)
"My Wife the Dancer."
Photo: Andrea Fell

(above right)
Lloyd in the 1994 show number
"Patricia the Stripper."

(left)
Isabelle in "Patricia the Stripper."

(above left) Isabelle and Lloyd with their coaches, Eric Gillies and Josée Picard at the 1994 World's in Japan. (above right) Isabelle and Rocky Marval on vacation in St. Lucia.

Isabelle and Lloyd, on his bike, in 1995.

The Brasseur & Eisler Star Lift. *Photo: Gérard Châtaigneau*

couldn't push or do anything. Isabelle said there was no way we could skate the next day but I told her I had to try.

We arrived at the rink on Sunday and attempted to do what we could. We skated very slowly and I kept one arm rigid. I pushed with one leg and Isabelle propelled me through all the elements we had to do. Although I was in a great deal of pain, we managed to finish the show but I realized that the work was just beginning if I wanted to make Nationals. I couldn't jump, and without the jumps we might as well stay home.

Isabelle

Lloyd was told he couldn't jump until a week before Nationals and it took a lot of adapting to train for this competition. We contacted Dr. Peter Jensen, who made up a schedule for us. He basically told us to take things one step at a time and we followed his schedule exactly.

The first time Lloyd stepped onto the ice, he was allowed twice around the rink and that was all. The next day, he was scheduled to skate around the rink twice forward and twice backward. If he was in a lot of pain and not able to follow Peter's plan, then he would repeat what he had done the previous day. As long as too much time didn't pass between each step, Lloyd would be able to begin jumping again a few days before Nationals. If there was too much of a delay in our training, we wouldn't be able to compete that year.

I trained on my own and we both did what was necessary to get us to Nationals. We just did the best we could and stayed very positive. Peter played a huge part in getting us through it.

Lloyd

Our training for Nationals was just as hard on Isabelle and our coaches as it was on me. They weren't absolutely convinced that I was going to be ready. Dr. Jensen came to help out. He had worked miracles for Isabelle and me in the past, getting us through our problems in 1989. He also had made up a schedule for Isabelle on how to perform the double Axel properly because it had been a barrier for her to get over. I had no reason not to trust him when he set up the same kind of schedule for me.

It was a day-by-day, session-by-session progression that I would have to make to compete at Nationals and, at the beginning, I just couldn't do anything. It was a good day if I was able to perform a single loop and some other pairs elements. Peter helped us tremendously to keep our minds on track of our goal, but I found it to be a long December and an even longer January.

Isabelle

I was a little nervous going into the 1991 Nationals. But I was mostly afraid for Lloyd. He had only begun jumping the week we were there and he was going to perform his first double Axel during the competition.

We knew we had to do well to make the World team. Just before the short program, he told me, "If I can't manage my jump, I'll do a single or just skip it altogether, but you keep going and do yours as best you can. We'll be deducted for it but it should be all right, since I'm sure I can do all the pairs elements."

I listened to what he had to say and thought it shouldn't be a problem. Over the last month, I had become used to not having him around me when I was jumping. I would just do my jump and whatever happened would happen. I knew he could do the pairs elements. That aspect wasn't like jumping and landing on his knee. It was an extra weight but an equal weight. I must admit, though, I was a little scared that he might drop me during the lifts. It had been so long since we had done a total run-through.

Lloyd

We arrived at the Nationals in Saskatoon without once having completely gone through our programs since my injury. I also hadn't performed a double jump in more than a month. My knee wasn't the only source of stress at this competition. The media had recently got hold of the story and were pressuring us for comments.

All eyes seemed to be on Isabelle and me during practices. Since I had to wear the brace on the outside of my pants, it was highly visible. It went from the top of my thigh right down to my ankle and was very cumbersome looking. I think everyone was wondering what I was doing out on the ice. For the competition, though, it would be on the inside of my costumes, which had been refitted. I was actually getting quite accustomed to the feel of the brace. It was made out of titanium and was very light.

We began our short program and it was the first time I was going to perform the double Axel. While Isabelle did hers flawlessly, I two-footed mine, but I don't think anyone noticed. We skated the rest of the program great and received a standing ovation.

The next night we did our long program and, much to everyone's surprise, we performed at the level that we should have been at without the injury and won the competition. When it was all over, I remember Isabelle saying, "Wow! If we can get through this, we can get through anything."

Isabelle

After Nationals, we went back to our usual way of training for Worlds. Everyone thought we may have a chance of winning, since Gordeeva and Grinkov had retired and we were number one in line.

We arrived in Munich, hopeful that this might be our chance, although Lloyd was still wearing the leg brace. After skating clean in the short, our optimism rose even higher as we sat in first.

During the long program, Lloyd did a single jump instead of a double but other than that we skated perfectly. There was only a small deduction for popping the jump but, as luck would have it, our main competitors, Dmitriev and Mishkutenok skated cleanly and the gold medal went to them while, once again, we took silver.

Lloyd

The media blitz was really on for Worlds, where everyone expected us to win. We were just trying to stay focused, though, because my knee was still a concern and I had again taken time off from jumping.

Practices went great in Munich. Both Josée and Eric were there since they had two teams competing. Jean-Michel Bombardier and his then partner, Stacey Ball, had come third at Nationals and had also qualified for Worlds.

After the short program, Isabelle and I were very excited to be sitting in first place and the Canadian media hype was just phenomenal. For the long, we had drawn near the last and were skating very well. In that program, we had a double Axel combination, which was the toughest jump for me to do with the brace on.

When Isabelle and I jump, people usually watch her. They figure that since she is not the stronger jumper of the pair, if one of us is going to miss it, it will be Isabelle. We headed into the combination jump and she did it perfectly, while I singled mine.

Because everyone had their attention on Isabelle, after our jump they clapped and cheered. Almost no one in the audience knew that I had popped the jump. Even some of the judges didn't notice and it wasn't until the television announcers replayed the jump that they caught it. But, because of my single, we came second and I was very disappointed to have let the team down. I was supposed to be the consistent one, the one who could do the jumps, and here Isabelle landed one perfectly and I missed mine at a very crucial time. It cost us a world championship.

Isabelle

Everyone drinks beer in Munich all the time. Even in the arena, there was a bar fifteen feet from the ice. The beer was free and the first thing the guys did after competing was to head there. Sometimes they still had their costumes on.

My parents had come to Munich and we were all excited about winning the silver. Things had really changed with my dad by then. He had started to work again that year, and although he was back into my skating, it was in a different way. After we had done well at Worlds in 1990, he realized that I could do it on my own, and from that point on it was *my* skating. He was there to support me and follow me, but it was *my* career.

In Munich, I also found that Dad was treating me more like an adult. We went to bars together to have a beer—it was as if he thought, She is old enough to drink with me. He was finally realizing that I was mature. One night, all the skaters went out on the town. By the time we got back to the hotel, it was 6:00 in the morning. We ran into my parents, who were on their way to eat breakfast. I was really proud of my dad, who didn't admonish me at all. He simply laughed and he and Mom went on about their business.

Lloyd

The Worlds had been great, and although I had been a little upset about missing my jump, I soon got over it and was happy with our silver. My parents had stayed about sixty miles outside of Munich, taking the train in every day to watch us. After that initial year of skating with Isabelle, my parents had become my biggest fans and supported me every way they could.

We were then off to tour Europe, where I performed the entire time wearing my leg brace. That was the first year we did our role reversal number, where I dressed up like a woman and Isabelle like a man. It was called "Henrietta" back then and our current "Patricia the Stripper" program evolved from that routine. People went crazy when we did it and we were discovering that we were making quite a name for ourselves in the show skating world.

The tour covered several countries, and although we didn't spend a great deal of time with each other, I think Isabelle enjoyed it. I know I did. In Switzerland, everyone except for me went skiing. There was no way I could maneuver the slopes with my knee, so instead I sat at the bottom of the hill, watching the others and drinking wine. I had a great time, merrily chatting away to anyone who wanted to listen.

While in Rome, we stayed at a small villa where the skaters occupied the majority of rooms. Kristi Yamaguchi was on this tour, and one night she drew a bath and ended up flooding the entire hotel. Apparently, the spout broke and water was shooting up into the air. I was one floor down and heard a trickling noise outside my door. It was very late and I had just left some of the others, who were still partying. Afraid to open the door in case someone was peeing against it, I stood and wondered what to do. It was only when water came seeping into the room that I opened the door and discovered a waterfall cascading down the stairwell.

Isabelle

I went skiing for the first time in my life on the European tour and visited countries that I had never seen before. Everyone was very relaxed because we had just finished Worlds, and it was a wonderful experience for me. There were only about twenty skaters and, unlike the Tom Collins tour, where people with different nationalities tend to stick together, everyone on this tour mixed with each other.

Lloyd and I had a few problems hanging around together, though, so he would usually be with his friends and I would be with mine. We had not dated for a while now but we still wanted and needed our own space.

We did five shows a week, and because we finished so late, by the time we returned from dinner it was at least 2:00 in the morning. I never slept in. Needless to say, I was exhausted when we got home and I slept for almost the entire two weeks before setting out on the Tom Collins tour.

Around this time, my partner and I were approached by various agents. Lloyd was quite eager but I wasn't too sure. It was never my goal to go professional. To me, skating was more sport than entertainment. My dream was to make it to the Olympics and, even after

I had accomplished that, I still didn't think about skating as a professional career.

Lloyd finally convinced me to sign with IMG, the world's largest sports marketing agency. But even my commitment to them didn't represent the start of a professional career to me. I believed the agency was there only to take care of the paperwork for us until we had finished with amateur skating. I really hadn't given much thought to what I wanted to do after that. Little did I know that my simplistic ideas would change so drastically in the future.

Lloyd

I had almost given up trying to acquire an agent. The year before, when I had looked for one, nobody was interested. Now, we had our choice of who we wanted to sign with. Isabelle and I discussed everything with Josée, who wasn't too enthusiastic about it. But I felt very strongly that it was a good move and so I pushed for it.

Isabelle was still pretty young and didn't know what to expect. I had friends who had agents, though, and saw all the things they were doing and the extra shows and the dollars they were making to help fund the skating.

Like Isabelle, I had never thought about skating professionally. Back then, there weren't many shows. Tom Collins was open only to amateurs and "Stars on Ice" toured very few cities at that time. The only venues left for professional skating were the "Ice Capades" or "Holiday on Ice." To be truthful, I figured once my amateur career was over, I would go back to university, earn a teaching certificate and become a physical education teacher. Funny how life has a way of changing things.

CHAPTER SIX

Losing Perspective

Lloyd

A WEEK after we arrived home from tour, I was in Toronto and at the hospital for surgery on my knee. Although I had been told the procedure was a relatively simple one, I was in no way prepared for what I saw upon awakening after the operation.

The bandages went all the way from midthigh to my toes and the spot where my knee was supposed to be was puffed up beyond belief. John came to pick me up to take me back to his and Pam's place to recuperate. He took one look and gasped, "What did they do to you . . . cut off your leg?"

I'd been advised that I would be off from eight to ten weeks for rehabilitation and then another two months before skating. But I knew I couldn't be away for that length of time. The year 1992 was an Olympic year and I wanted to be ready. There was no way I was going to listen to the doctors and I started disobeying their orders immediately. "Leave the bandages on for a week," they had sternly warned. But I wasn't home fifteen minutes before I started unwinding them and, within the hour, was doing exercises.

About a week after the surgery, John was heading up to Sault Ste. Marie to see his family, and since I was off for the summer anyway, I thought I might as well join him. One day I overheard John and some of the others planning a golf game. They were surprised when I announced I wanted to play as well. I had brought my clubs, anticipating just such an opportunity. "How can you possibly play?" they asked. But I had it all worked out.

"We will get a drive cart and I will just stand up to hit the ball and then get back in the cart," I explained. Everyone thought I was crazy but decided to humor "the patient." I guess my athletics were quite the sight as I climbed out of the golf cart, stabilized myself, hit the ball and then climbed back in. The group's laughter quickly turned into irritation after I won the game.

The rest of the summer was spent in therapy for three or four days a week while Isabelle trained on her own. By mid-August, I thought I'd give skating a try and was back on the ice a month early, although I still required the leg brace for support. I knew I should probably give my knee more healing time but I was eager to get the 1992 season under way.

Isabelle

When Lloyd and I finally got together on the ice, it was slow getting back to normal. He couldn't jump for a while and so we concentrated on the choreography for our new programs, going again to Delaware to work with Uschi. Our short program was skated to can-can music and the long program was set to a medley of very upbeat, contemporary pieces. It's funny, but up until 1992 Nationals, I have a hard time remembering competing with those programs. We had done so many fall competitions in the past, and would do many more in the future, that many of them have now become quite hazy in my memory.

Lloyd

I guess the biggest controversy of the fall for us centered on the white outfits we wore for the long program. Josée had always designed our costumes and this year was no exception. They were considered to be rather wild, covered from top to bottom with bugle beads of all different colors. We were very pleased with them and everyone around us thought they looked good, yet we had an entirely different opinion from the judges. They hated them. "Too contemporary. Too over the edge," were the comments that filtered back to us and, above all it seems, they didn't like white.

In my opinion, the reason the judges disliked them was that we hadn't yet joined many of our peers, who spent a lot of money and hired big, fancy designers to create their outfits. In the political world of skating, Josée was considered a coach, not a designer. Besides, one of the top designers was also a judge. You figure it out.

We refused to give in to their opinions though and wore these costumes. In fact, just before Nationals, we arranged to have more beading sewn on, making the costumes even splashier. It was our way of thumbing our noses at the system.

Trophée Lalique was to be our first international competition that fall but we had to withdraw because my leg wasn't ready. A week later, we were at Nations Cup in Germany. I barely landed a couple of jumps. My knee was sore and I was still wearing the brace, but despite it all, we came first and it was a huge boost to our confidence.

While we were at Nations Cup, I received some devastating news. Rob McCall had died from AIDS, and although he had been ill for quite a while, his death was still a shock. We flew home and I drove to Toronto for his funeral, where the skating world had gathered to pay tribute to this wonderful man. Dr. Jensen delivered the eulogy and, later, a close group of friends gathered at Brian Orser's place. We reminisced about the great times we had spent with our friend and I believe the casual setting was in character with what Rob believed life should be.

It bothered me to see how the public and media were coming down hard on our sport during this time. This disease extended far beyond the figure skating world but attention seemed to be focusing on the sport and connecting the two. I had lost a close friend and that was sad, but people's ignorance was the truly tragic issue.

Because we felt we needed the practice, we did Divisionals that year and, to our surprise, received a 6.0 for artistic impression for the first time in our career. It was extremely gratifying because we had always been called the "technical wonders," and until then no one had commented on how far we had come artistically.

The day after Christmas, we performed in Montreal as guest stars in the "Ice Capades." I had quit my job after the 1990 tour, and to help pay for our skating, Isabelle and I were taking on more exhibitions and shows.

It was a little strange for me that year, though, since it was my first Christmas away from home. The Eislers were always a very traditional family, and each holiday season we made a point of gathering in Seaforth. Because this show required Isabelle and I to be on the ice at 9:30 the next morning, it was impossible for me to spend Christmas Day at home. That wasn't easy for me or my parents.

Isabelle

On January 11, 1992, my grandpa passed away. It was the first time that someone close to me had died. He had been rushed to the hospital with what doctors thought was a hernia, but when they began to operate, they realized that his internal organs were paralyzed. The medical team just closed him up and Grandpa never really woke up after that.

He passed away the day we were leaving for Nationals, which was being held early since it was an Olympic year. I stayed behind but everyone in my family urged me to leave and join the other skaters in Moncton. They said that was what Grandpa would have wanted. I gave in to their wishes and left for the competition the next day but my heart wasn't in it. I felt that I shouldn't be skating, and missing my grandpa's funeral made me very sad.

Once we began competing, my mind just wasn't there and we skated terribly in the short program—both of us. I missed the double Axel, and when we were in the middle of a pairs spin, Lloyd fell.

When done correctly, the spin we were doing is beautiful: Lloyd's leg is above me and I am almost lying down as we spin. I believe it was the only time we missed a spin during a competition. The long program went better and we won Nationals, but while I was skating, I kept thinking about my grandpa and how I should have been at home.

Lloyd

I thought we were ready for Nationals. We had trained well and my knee was presenting few problems by then. Although I wasn't playing hockey yet, I was able to skate without the brace. During the short program, however, we were doing a new spin that put us in a position that was hard on my knee. I pulled too hard and in the process yanked my feet out from under me, causing the two of us to fall. Isabelle, who was going through a bad time with the loss of her grandfather, had missed her jump as well. So in two minutes and forty seconds, we had fallen twice—not one of our more stellar performances, I'd say.

After we received the marks, which put us second, I walked into the dressing room fuming at myself because I had fallen on a pairs spin. I picked up a chair and hurled it across the room, where it smashed into the wall. There were many other skaters around and they just stood back and watched my outburst in amazement. I was so frustrated because we had been skating well prior to Nationals.

My father had driven the seventeen hours from Ontario to see me compete and I was glad he was there. He told me not to worry about the way we had skated, reminding me that the top three teams would go to the Olympics. He also thought we would do much better in the long. Dad was right. Isabelle and I went out, skated beautifully and reclaimed the Canadian championship.

Isabelle

I absolutely hated life at home during the weeks leading up to the Olympics. There was just too much pressure. Everyone tried to make us feel good but many comments had the opposite effect. For example, Lloyd and I would be in a restaurant and someone would come over and say, "Bring back the gold."

My stomach would immediately become tied in knots as I thought, Thanks for reminding me. I have just finished training for five hours, am trying to relax and forget about things and now you have told me that I have to win the gold! I know that is not what people meant but at the time that is how I took it.

When the media called for interviews, we were unable to refuse and began to get distracted. After a while, I just stayed home and hibernated to avoid the questions and comments. I realized people were only attempting to encourage us and, of course, were not purposely trying to apply pressure. But because I had no experience with this kind of stress and didn't have a clue how to deal with it, I found the situation to be almost unbearable.

Lloyd

Because we had come second at Worlds the year before, and won Nations Cup and then the Canadian championships, people started to believe we were going to the Olympics for one reason—to win gold. But that was not our intention . . . or it hadn't been up to that point. Our original goal was to skate well and hopefully be on the podium. The media and the public just couldn't understand our attitude. They thought we should prepare to claim the top prize.

There was so much pressure. Every day between Nationals and the Olympics television people called, wanting more interviews. There were forms to fill out and team send-offs and banquets to attend—we found it difficult to focus on our training. Isabelle and I tried to stick to our game plan and trained well in spite of the distractions. When we arrived in Albertville, France, we believed we were as ready as we could be.

Isabelle

Even though my entire family was there to support me, I didn't feel the same excitement that I had felt in Calgary. Lloyd and I were now the oldest pair on the team. I was far more mature and confident than I had been at the last Olympics.

Going against tradition, our team suits were white and purple and that seemed a little strange to everyone. Not being in our usual and very identifiable red and white colors caused many Canadian athletes to say we didn't look like the Canadian team.

The 1992 Olympics was one of the worst organized events ever and I don't have a lot of good things to say about it. Our village was one of five and was located at scenic Bride-les-Bain. Because of the mountains and poor roads, which were sometimes reduced to a single lane of traffic, the venues were two or three hours away by bus. And the food in the village was terrible! Can you imagine being in France and not enjoying the cuisine?

One fun way to pass the time was sending electronic mail through the computer system, which athletes lined up to use. Many of my messages were to Jean-Luc Brassard, a freestyle skier I had met the previous summer at a boat race in his hometown. The Brassard family held a barbecue afterwards at their house and over the next few months, Jean-Luc and I became friends. In the near future, our relationship was to develop beyond friendship, but in Albertville we were still getting to know each other.

Lloyd

I thought Albertville was a great city. Our village was a long way from the venue so every day we had an hour and a half on the bus, where I usually passed the time sleeping. My roommate in the chalet-style house was Michael Slipchuk and across the hall were Kurt Browning and Doug Ladret.

Every practice, Isabelle and I skated clean, perfect programs and the buzz around was that we were almost sure to win. We tried not to take notice but it took some effort to keep it all tuned out. In hindsight, I'm not sure we were successful.

The day after the opening ceremonies, Isabelle and I were on the ice for the short program, feeling extremely confident as we began. Then, Isabelle missed a double Axel. We'll never know why she missed it as she had nailed the jump all week in practice. We came around and she was almost crying, saying, "I blew it. I ruined it." There were still many elements left in the program and I tried to convince her not to worry about it.

"Let's just keep going to the end with lots of facial expression," I urged. "We can cry when we get off the ice but now let's put the artistic value into the program. There are six elements left. Let's make them wonder if we really missed that jump." Talking to each other all the way through the rest of the program, we managed to keep big smiles on our faces. But as soon as the music stopped, reality set in.

Isabelle

When I got on the ice, I thought I could do it. Practices had been good and we were feeling sure of ourselves, but the next thing I knew, I was on my butt after the double Axel. I lay there for a split second and my mind raced . . . Okay, get up, I thought. Is this a dream? Pinch me. Did I really fall here? Yes, I fell. Oh my God, we are at the Olympics and I've blown it.

As we continued with the program, I remember Lloyd encouraging me to smile but I had such a hard time. I had fallen on one of the first elements and was thinking, Why should I pretend to be happy? I ruined it. All of our hopes fell when I did and I didn't see why I should smile and keep trying. But Lloyd was adamant.

"Okay," he said. "Six more elements. Come on. You can do it." He was so good with me. Yes, he was as disappointed as I was, but on the ice he did everything he could to help me get through it.

Coming off, I was devastated and when I made it to the dressing room, I wept in Josée's arms. "I can't believe I fell and let everyone down," I cried. She tried to console me but I could see the sadness in her face.

Lloyd

I bowed and skated off with my arm around Isabelle, who kept repeating, "I'm sorry. I'm sorry I missed the jump."

"Don't worry about it," I said nonchalantly. "It's not your fault. We miss it . . . so we miss it." Although I was trying to maintain an air of calm, inside I was angry. I wasn't upset with Isabelle. I was more bummed that we had put so much work into training this year, skated so well at practices and then missed it during the program. It was just so disheartening.

There were a lot of tears that night but Isabelle had her family there to support her, while I had only Dr. Jensen and our coaches. My parents had been unable to attend because everything was very expensive in Albertville and, to be perfectly frank, we couldn't afford it.

After we got off the ice, I remember going outside for a long walk. The temperature was at least minus twenty but, with the mood I was in, the cold somehow escaped me. We had skated at the beginning and I didn't want to watch anyone else, needing this time to be alone. I figured, with our fall, we would probably be sixth or seventh when all was said and done.

When I finally went back in, to my surprise we were sitting third. Apparently Dmitriev and Mishkutenok had skated well, along with Bechke and Petrov, but no one else had. Isabelle and I suddenly became very lucky. I think, too, that the effort we had put into the artistic value from the time of the fall until the end gave the illusion that we were having a great program in spite of our error. If we hadn't have put on that facade, it would have been easy to run our program into the ground and blow our chances at a medal.

Isabelle

The next day, I was still downhearted and a part of me wondered why I should even continue to try. At the same time, a voice from within offered encouragement.

During the long program, I heard those two little voices in my head all the time. One of them was saying, Oh come on, just quit. It is not worth it. The other kept repeating, Hey you, fight it! You're in third place. Don't let go. You still have a chance.

Those two voices are all I can remember about that program. Don't ask me what mistakes I made. I only recall the fight going on inside me and then skating off the ice feeling so very sad.

Lloyd

At practice, we skated outstandingly and just before our long program, we had a great warm-up. Then came the competition. We went out and on our first element, which was a throw—boom, Isabelle fell. From there, we performed some things well and other things badly. It was an average program with another fall toward the end and both Isabelle and I were extremely disappointed.

I remember sitting in the "kiss and cry" area, where television cameras catch the reactions of skaters to their scores, and feeling very dejected, thinking that we were going to drop to fourth. I had come all this way to another Olympics and things hadn't worked out. When the marks came up, reflecting our poor performance, I left before I should have. I felt as if we had failed but I wasn't blaming my partner. We are a team. *We* missed something. In Nationals, I had fallen and Isabelle had taken the brunt of it and now she had fallen. All I knew was that I had to get away.

There was a big hullabaloo over my behavior. Everyone said later that they couldn't believe I would leave Isabelle sitting there by herself. I took a beating from the media and the association; both stated how inconsiderate I had been. They thought I was concerned only about myself.

It wasn't that I didn't care about Isabelle. I have always worn my emotions on my sleeve and expressed my thoughts honestly. I was upset and I left. I just didn't want to be there. My leaving certainly had nothing to do with Isabelle and my feelings toward her. Anyone who would believe that I blamed Isabelle just doesn't know how deep our relationship is.

Isabelle

I felt pretty bad when Lloyd walked away. Because I am so tough on myself, I already felt depressed and thought that even my best friend was ashamed of me. I took his leaving very personally and remember thinking how much I wanted to get out of this sport, which was making me so unhappy. I figured there must be other things in life that were not as much pressure and were not as physically difficult. I felt so disgraced and the little confidence I had left became nonexistent.

About half an hour later, Lloyd came to me and said, "Don't worry. We will try again next time. We'll go back and figure out what happened." I asked him why he had walked away and if he was indeed ashamed of me. He explained that was not the way he felt at all. I accepted what he said and, under the circumstances, things were as good as they could be between us, but it took me a while to forgive and forget the incident.

My dad was also discouraged. But a friend of the family took him aside and said, "Hey, your daughter is third at the Olympics! Be proud for once. Be happy." He came around a little but everyone's somber reaction bothered me because I thought it was my fault. Although they did their best to comfort me, it was too late because of the shame I was feeling. They couldn't fix that, no matter what they said. Nobody could change the way I felt about myself. I just wanted to go home.

Lloyd

Four days after the opening ceremonies, we were done and had close to two weeks to kick around in Albertville. I was still feeling down about our third-place finish and someone suggested that maybe we should go home and train for Worlds. But there was no way that I was coming to the Olympics, whether I had skated well or not, and missing the rest of the Games. I wanted to see everything.

For the remaining time, I enjoyed myself a little too much, as Kris Wirtz, Doug Ladret, a few of the bobsledders and I took in all the sights. On the day of the closing ceremonies, some of us went to the final hockey game. I wasn't drunk but had a few too many beers and was sporting a red, yellow and orange clown's wig that I thought added a certain something to my team uniform.

The hockey players had told us to come down after the game and they would give us sticks as souvenirs. I was sitting with Chris Lorri, who said he would go and that I should wait for him in the stands. Well, I waited and waited and waited. The arena was empty and "Houdini," as he is more commonly known, had disappeared.

I was in Mirabelle, forty-five minutes from the site of the closing ceremonies, which were due to start in an hour, and I had no way of getting there. Luckily, I was able to hitch a ride on a bus that was carrying the ladies' curling team and made it just in time. My wig and knapsack full of beer didn't seem to bother them at all.

When I arrived, the Canadian team was already lining up to march into the stadium. I saw Houdini, who swore that he had told me to meet him outside. He hadn't, but I soon forgave him because he handed me an autographed hockey stick that belonged to Sean Burke, our goalie.

When I finally caught up with Isabelle, I said, "Well, I made it. Let's go." She took one look at my wig, my knapsack and hockey stick and asked me if I was going in like that. When I replied that I was, she said, "Goodbye," and proceeded to walk in with another group.

After the ceremonies were finished, we strolled over to one of the arenas that was housing a huge party. At this point the various teams had broken up and everyone was mingling with each other in true Olympic style.

The arena was decorated with about thirty red, blue and white banners, about forty feet long and hanging from the ceiling. I noticed a couple of guys trying to pull one down, and since I was taller, I reached up and gave it a good yank and it came fluttering to the ground. They thanked me for my help but I said, "No, no, no. I just showed you how to get it down. This one is mine," and then very quickly I took another one. Everyone in the building joined in and, within ten seconds, all the banners were gone. It was like dominos. They just fell and disappeared. I wound up with three in total. I kept two and donated the third to the arena in Seaforth. It hangs there now, running the length of the rink, with a huge picture of Isabelle and me and a congratulatory message to us for winning the bronze medal.

Even though I had such a good time for the remainder of the Games, the turmoil I felt about the way we had skated didn't go away quickly and I just couldn't enjoy winning the bronze. In retrospect, I realize that obtaining a medal of any color at the Olympics is a feat in itself.

What happened to Kurt Browning is a perfect example of this. Everything was on him to win but Kurt didn't medal at all, which was even more discouraging for him. He had been World champion and had headed to the Olympics with a great chance of winning the gold. Kurt skated poorly while everyone else skated well and he finished with nothing. Isabelle and I had not skated as well as we usually do, but because others skated just as poorly, we received a bronze. Eventually, we learned how to accept what had happened to us, but back then the frustrations of not competing well and the stress that accompanied it interfered with all logical thought.

Isabelle

A few days after we competed, I was in the bedroom with my family when Kurt came walking in. He hadn't yet competed and we all had high hopes for him. Taking a look at my medal, which was lying on the bed, Kurt said, "Hey, this is great!"

I assumed he was just trying to cheer me up and responded with a lackluster, "Yeah . . . well."

"What more could you ask for?" he continued. "To win a medal at the Olympics is pretty fantastic. I wish I could get one." My dad told him to try it on and then Kurt asked us to take his picture. "Boy," he said as he inspected the medal, "I can't wait until I have one too."

After he competed and didn't do well, I felt so bad for Kurt. We wanted to console him but he left for home immediately. It was then I began to realize that maybe it wasn't all that easy to win a medal and that, yes, it was normal to be nervous at an event like this. We are only human and can't be perfect all the time.

Upon making this realization, I became determined to enjoy the rest of the Games, and aside from the way we had skated, this Olympics turned out to be my best. I went skiing and attended as many events as possible, including Jean-Luc's competition. Unfortunately, he didn't do well either and came seventh.

I roomed with Josée Chouinard, who arrived three days after I had finished competing. She must have found it difficult watching me have such a good time while she was trying to concentrate on skating. But we still managed to have fun together and I tried to respect what she was going through.

Because we had trouble getting to Albertville, many of the athletes began to frequent a tiny bar just outside our village. It was called "Le Phoque," which means "The Seal." Obviously, I can't pronounce it for you but, trust me, the French version sounds very similar to an English word that isn't supposed to be used in mixed company.

That place became an ongoing joke: people would say that they were going to "Le Phoque" or they would meet you at "Le Phoque." We laughed every time we said or heard it. The bar was very small, and because everyone would eventually wind up there after their day's outing, it was usually overflowing. The owner did pretty well too. By the end of the week he didn't have any alcohol left—he just ran out.

One night, a group of us went to Albertville and, later on, I found I didn't have a ride home. Public transportation was terrible and I tried to avoid it at all costs. During the second week, I had gone to see Jean-Luc and come back by bus: it took me four hours. As luck would have it on that night, though, I met a group of bobsledders who were also looking for a ride.

We hired a man with a truck and paid him to drive us. I was the only girl squashed in the back of this old truck with all these guys but it was fun. Those bobsledders had a great sense of humor, kidding around all the way. When we arrived at the village, we discovered we didn't have enough money to pay the agreed-upon price. The man began to argue but when all eight of these very large bobsledders descended from the truck, looked him up and down and said, "What's the problem?" the driver soon made a hasty retreat.

On the day of the closing ceremonies, we went to see a hockey game. All the skaters jumped into the bus right after the game—except for Lloyd. I began to panic, thinking he was going to miss the ceremonies. At that time, we believed this would be our last Olympics and I knew how much it meant for him to be there.

Just before we were going to march into the stadium, I heard a loud voice calling me. "Fred! Where are you, Fred?" There was Lloyd at the back of the group, still wearing his wig. I looked at him and thought, Oh my God . . . do I know this person? I decided then and there that my partner could walk in by himself.

Lloyd

On the way home after the Olympics, the reality of the situation hit us and we were both feeling very pessimistic. We didn't want to train for Worlds or do anything else, for that matter, and the fact that Isabelle and I weren't getting along didn't help.

We weren't really fighting but the communication we usually had just wasn't there and we constantly debated whether we should even bother with Worlds. In our eyes, we hadn't skated well at the Olympics and we wondered if we should just quit.

While we ran this notion through our minds, Isabelle and I weren't training very hard—we were just going through the motions. We had busted our butts before the Olympics and had been skating well right up to the competition. What difference would it make now if we worked hard? Our chance to shine had disappeared.

Three or four days before we were scheduled to leave for Oakland, California, Isabelle and I finally made up our minds to participate. We would compete and then quit after the 1992 Worlds.

Isabelle

When we arrived back in Quebec, everybody from the club was at the airport to greet us. They apparently thought it was amazing that we had won a medal at the Olympics because we were the first figure skaters from the province to do so. Their warm welcome made me feel good.

At first, we weren't even sure if we wanted to compete at Worlds and I found it very tough to train. But once we had decided to go, I tried to keep the attitude that we had only two more weeks of skating and so I might as well make the best of them. Our main goal now was to finish the season on a good note.

Both of our families came to Oakland, and for the entire week prior to the competition we maintained the same outlook: Let's just try and make this one better. I figured if I fell, then I fell. It couldn't be worse than the Olympics and we had nothing to lose. Even with this attitude, though, we had a rough time at some of the practices, yet we tried to remain positive.

For the short program, we skated first and did well. After we received our marks, I remember my dad blowing me kisses from above the "kiss and cry" area and shouting, "Good job, good job . . . good girl, good girl!" He was so happy that I had skated well. We remained in first place for a long time. Then Dmitriev and

Mishkutenok skated their program, and although they made an error, the judges put them ahead of us. Lloyd wasn't too pleased.

Lloyd

Isabelle and I went out for the short program and skated perfectly. Then, Natalia Mishkutenok two-footed her double Axel and, of the nine judges, only one saw it. When their marks came up, all were 5.9's except for one 5.5. The American judge had been the only one to catch their mistake. A few minutes before, I had been so happy— now I was angry. They had won gold in Albertville and rightly so, but in Oakland they didn't deserve to win the short program and should have come in third or fourth.

It was east versus west coming back to haunt us and I was mad. I said to Isabelle, "See that? We skate well and it doesn't matter. We're still not going to get the marks." Of course, the whole incident really brought us down. The two of us were fed up with skating at that point. We had done our job this time but were not going to be rewarded accordingly. It was all politics, as usual.

The night of the long program, we began and Isabelle hit the double Axel perfectly. We were on a roll and continued to skate well. Then, about halfway through the program, she fell on the triple Salchow but it was no big deal. She got up and we kept going, having already landed one throw and the side-by-side jumps. I was thinking, we made only one mistake . . . not a bad program. There were thirty seconds left when Isabelle fell on our last element. It was a jump that she had probably not missed once in her entire life. And, unfortunately, a fall at the end of a program really sets the mood.

We came off the ice with long faces and sat down to receive the marks. They were terrible and once again I walked away. I was just so tired after the last month and a half. Out of the four programs we had performed, we had finally skated one perfectly and didn't receive the marks for it. It was so discouraging for me. We dropped to third behind Kovarikova and Novotny, who placed second. Mishkutenok and Dmitriev again won the gold.

I recall going out for the presentation of the medals that night and not feeling too chipper. As we stood on the podium, Isabelle looked at me and told me she was finished with skating. I said, "Let's not talk about it now. Just smile." But we look at those podium pictures now and Isabelle is not smiling at all.

Isabelle

In the long program, we started out well. Then I missed one throw and that little mistake brought my confidence level down. Then we performed a combination jump and I missed it too.

When I came off the ice, I was so angry with myself, I acted very negatively. I began to cry and then Josée became upset too. Because we had performed strongly in the short, we came third, but that was no consolation to me. I remember standing on the podium and being so mean to Lloyd. I said, "Enjoy this one because this is your last. I am never going to be back up here again."

He looked at me in surprise and said, "Pardon me?"

"You heard properly," I shot back. I guess, in my head, it was the end of my career. I'd had enough.

To add to my misery, I was selected for the doping test and had to stay behind. My mom and dad waited for me and drove me back to the hotel. Dad was so unhappy to see me this depressed that he began to cry too. He said, "I'm sorry for putting you in this sport and for making you cry like this. I never wanted that. Please don't be angry with me." He blamed himself that I was so miserable and felt guilty about the fact that he had always encouraged me to skate and had constantly pushed me to do better.

When we arrived back at the hotel, a woman on the Canadian team talked to me and my dad. I can't recall who it was but I do remember what she said. She asked me why I was so sad and I told her that it was because I felt ashamed of myself. People expected me to do it and I just couldn't.

She replied, "You are only twenty-one years old. Think about all you have done in life and all you have accomplished. You may not be proud of yourself right now but think about how much more you have experienced and how much further ahead you are than other people who are much older than you."

Then she said to my dad, "How would you like to have been Isabelle's age and done everything she has? Your daughter has already achieved so much in life." I guess her speech had an effect on both of us because, after Worlds, Dad and I talked at great length about my career. One day he said, "If you want to keep skating, it's up to you. But if you feel like getting out of the sport, we will understand and help you with whatever you choose. If you work as hard as you have with your skating, you will do just fine."

I thought long and hard about what I wanted to do after Worlds. My first inclination was to stop skating immediately, but I decided to do the tour. I would quit after that.

Lloyd

Isabelle was very unhappy and down on herself after Worlds, but as far as I was concerned, it was starting to sink in that we had a bronze medal from the Olympics and another bronze from Worlds and maybe that wasn't so bad.

One of the teams had dropped from second at the Olympics to sixth at Worlds. Another team didn't win a medal at the Olympics but were now second at Worlds. Dmitriev and Mishkutenok and Isabelle and I were the only teams that had stayed in the top three positions over the two competitions. That was a pretty fair accomplishment.

I tried to explain this to Isabelle but she wasn't listening. Her ears were blocked at this point and she wasn't paying any attention to what I was saying. We decided to go on tour and not talk about it anymore. That was easier said than done, though, since the next Olympics was only two years away. We were constantly being asked if we were going to quit or continue until 1994.

That year, the combined Tom Collins and isu tour hit about forty cities throughout North America. It was tough at first because we really didn't want to be there, but we soon found ourselves again enjoying the entertainment aspect of our skating.

This was our third year on the tour and people were starting to recognize our names and expect good performances from us. They had been particularly fond of the role reversal routine from the previous year and many expressed their desire to see it again, but Isabelle and I didn't want to repeat an old number. We instead came up with "Devil with the Blue Dress" and found the response to be fantastic.

It was on that tour that I discovered how solid a following Isabelle and I had and something clicked inside me. It was a desire not only to continue skating and perhaps realize some of our original goals but also to continue to develop our unique exhibition numbers. I was satisfied with my decision but now wondered how on earth I could convince Isabelle.

Isabelle

The tour went well and things seemed a little brighter to me. I could have done without the accident, though.

We were performing a new number that we had done only once before. In it, we slide on our knees across the ice at full speed. We are apart from each other and Lloyd follows me. During the performance, he was a little too close to where my hand was resting on the ice and he kicked me with his foot. I knew that he had touched me but I didn't feel a thing. In the next move, we raise our hands above our heads. At that moment, I noticed something flinging around and wondered, What was that? I looked at my hand and it was wide open. Lloyd had cut me with his skate.

The injury started at my pinky and continued to the middle finger, encompassing almost half of my left hand. The next element in our program was a spin and I was supposed to be in a backward position but was going forward. Lloyd yelled, "Spin, spin!" figuring that I had forgotten the program: he had no idea that I'd been cut.

"I can't," I said and showed him the gash. He stopped immediately and grabbed my hand to apply pressure. We then proceeded to walk the entire length of the ice to the exit, with no one in the audience realizing what had happened. When the producers saw my hand, they announced an intermission. It took about twelve stitches to close the wound.

After the tour, Lloyd told me that he wanted to continue skating for another two years because he didn't believe we had accomplished all that we should and could have. Since the announcement had been made that the next Olympics would be held in 1994, he thought we now had another opportunity to achieve some of our dreams.

We decided to take a month off, and although I didn't think that I wanted to skate anymore, I told Lloyd that I would give it serious thought. If I had had to make the decision right then and there, I would have probably said no. That's how much I wanted out of skating.

CHAPTER SEVEN

Insight Through Sorrow

Isabelle

DURING the next month I did a lot of soul searching because I wanted to be very sure of my decision. I spent many hours with Josée, who told me that if we wanted to try again, she and Eric would be there for us.

I asked her, "Do you believe that we can do it for another two years? Do you really think we have the potential?" and, more importantly, "Are you willing to stand behind Lloyd and I, no matter what happens?"

Once our coaches affirmed they were willing to support us one hundred percent, I began to feel better but was still unable to make a total commitment. I knew we would have to change our attitudes to succeed and learn how to cope with the pressure of competition. There was no way I could face another Olympics under the same circumstances.

I also acknowledged that I had been having a difficult time with our training. Lloyd's and my methods were so different. If I fell, I wanted to get up and try again—to Lloyd, it was a one shot deal. In my opinion, he never trained enough for me. He always thought that if you believe in yourself, you can do it when it's time. That method didn't work for me as I preferred to practice whatever I was having trouble with over and over again. If I was going to continue to skate, that problem would have to be resolved as well.

Since Lloyd was recuperating from another knee operation, I had plenty of time to think and didn't bother training on my own as I had the previous summer. I just wanted to be positive that if I persevered with my career, I would feel happy about skating again.

Lloyd

I guess after the last surgery I had started training too soon, not allowing my knee to heal properly. So when I arrived home from the tour, I returned to the hospital for more surgery. This time, I followed the doctor's orders to the letter. I was back on the ice later than I hoped but in much better shape.

In the meantime, Isabelle and I had many discussions about what we were going to do and came to one conclusion. Changes would have to be made. Josée didn't want us to quit, believing we would succeed if our perspective toward skating could be altered. She advised Isabelle and me how we should have reacted to winning our bronze medals and I began to feel terrible that we hadn't been appreciative.

Isabelle finally agreed to continue skating and we decided that, apart from the obvious changes in attitudes, we would also consider some of the CFSA's past suggestions. We weren't about to bow down to every criticism they had ever made but we were willing to compromise. The association believed that we should take the emphasis off the athletics in our programs and concentrate on the artistic side. Generally, they wanted us to appear more traditional and balletic. Although I wasn't entirely comfortable with their viewpoint, Isabelle and Josée liked their ideas, so we started over.

It was then I insisted that if we were going to do this, Isabelle and I would have to make a firm commitment for another two years, with no talk of quitting. There would be no giving up this time.

Isabelle

While I was trying to sort out my future, I needed something outside my sport to distract me from my troubles. I just wanted to laugh and be carefree again—I found what I was searching for in Jean-Luc Brassard.

We began to date that summer, and although our relationship was not what you would call serious, it was perfect for what I needed at the time. Jean-Luc is a very funny person and going out with him was so relaxing for me. It was pure enjoyment and if, for some reason, Jean-Luc wasn't there the next morning, that would be okay. But when he was there, I had a wonderful time and didn't worry about anything else.

I did things with Jean-Luc that I had never done before. There was a waterfall behind his house and, if the mood struck, we would simply jump in. Other times, we went canoeing or played like children on his trampoline. His family life was different from mine and I liked the escape from my routine. Our relationship was the only thing that kept me going that summer . . . the only thing that brought a smile to my face. Thanks to Jean-Luc, I was looking forward to life again.

Lloyd

In September, I had one last operation but this time it was on the other knee to repair torn cartilage. I wasn't able to skate for at least a month and so we didn't enter any competitions in the early fall. Instead, we were concentrating on our new look.

For the first time, Josée didn't design our costumes. We went to Frances Dafoe in Toronto, who had previously made outfits for the National Ballet and "Stars on Ice." She had also designed for a number of well-known skaters including Brian Orser, Kurt Browning and Underhill and Martini. That move was our first step in having the judges lean in our favor, since Frances was also going to be one of the pairs judges at the 1993 Worlds.

Our short program was skated to "Tequila" while the long was to a piece by Paganini. We had switched to classical music but used contemporary arrangements. At this point, I wasn't entirely happy with how the program would look. It was a drastic change for me. All of a sudden, Isabelle was the main focus and we developed the number around her elegance and softness. I was to remain powerful, but in the background and this was something that I was going to have to learn to do.

Isabelle

We sat down and tried to figure out what had gone wrong with our competitions that year. Why could we skate our programs so well in practice and then have such a hard time when we competed? We concluded that our practices were missing all the extras such as costumes, makeup, hair, judges and people in the stands. That was the difference, so we decided to begin simulating competitions.

We would put our costumes on and I would do my hair and makeup. Sometimes we would invite judges, have an audience and even ask other skaters to participate. We would warm up and then we would each do our programs. It was our hope that, when it came time for the real thing, we would think of the competition as just another practice session, eliminating some of the pressure.

Lloyd

I wasn't too keen on the simulations we did that fall, but knew they were necessary for the team to improve. Isabelle and Josée suggested the idea and it was done more for my partner's sake because she learns through repetition. Isabelle loves to do more and more and I don't.

In early November, we were scheduled to perform in a show called "The Jimmy Fund," which raises money for cancer research. It is held at Harvard University in Boston and was usually a huge party because everyone in the show stays on campus in the dorms with the students. We always had a great time.

It was a Friday night and Isabelle and I had just finished performing our first number. During intermission someone with a grave look on his face approached me and said that Dominique was on the phone. He wanted to speak to me.

Isabelle and I looked at each other in puzzlement, finding it unusual that her brother would be calling me. I took off my skates, went to the phone and listened as a very upset Dominique insisted that Isabelle be sent home right away.

Isabelle

Whenever I went out of town, as soon as I arrived at the airport, I would call my parents to let them know where I was going and when I'd be home.

We were on our way to do a show in Boston and at the terminal I went to make my usual call. I had a hard time finding a telephone and almost missed my flight. When I finally tracked one down and called, my dad answered. They were at work and I told him that I didn't have a long time to talk. I let him know where I was going and we wished each other a good weekend. I informed him that mine was probably going to be tiring because we had four shows to do.

He commented, "It is not the shows that make you tired. It is whatever goes on after." I assured him that I would try to get to bed early and he laughingly replied, "Sure, at Harvard University . . . I somehow doubt you'll be sleeping much." I told him I would see him on Sunday and hung up. If only I had known what was going to happen, I would never have boarded that plane.

Lloyd

At first, Dominique wouldn't say what was wrong but I knew from his voice that it must be something serious. I informed him that I just couldn't tell Isabelle that she had to go home without knowing what was going on. He finally told me that his dad had had a heart attack and agreed that I should have Isabelle call him back at their parents' place.

Isabelle

When Lloyd went to speak to Dominique, I went into the dressing room with an uneasy feeling. After a few minutes, I could hear Lloyd calling my name. "Fred, come here," he said and took me aside. "Your dad is not feeling well. You should go back tonight."

I phoned home and Dominique's wife, Josée, picked it up. She said that my mom and brother were at the hospital with my dad. I asked her what to do and she said that I'd better return immediately.

Lloyd

Because of the late hour, there were no flights out that night. A couple of students with a van said they would take Isabelle to Montreal. I wanted to go with her and offered to do the driving. I figured that the students might have to head right back and would be too tired to drive both ways.

After arrangements had been hastily made, I turned to Isabelle and said, "Let's go," but she refused, wanting to do the second number.

She was firm in her answer. "No," she replied. "We have made a commitment. We are here now and can't do anything about what is going on at home. Let's finish the show and then leave."

Isabelle

During the five-hour drive, Lloyd advised me to try to sleep, but every time I closed my eyes, I had an image of my dad passed away. At one point, I jumped up quickly and Lloyd asked me what was the matter. I told him I had a bad feeling but he kept reassuring me that everything would be fine. How I wanted to believe him.

We were supposed to go straight home, but somehow we got lost and ended up closer to the hospital than to my parents' house. Although it was 3:00 in the morning, I wanted to go in anyway, figuring my mom and Dominique would be there. I looked in the parking lot for their cars but couldn't see them. I thought that was strange but Lloyd said that maybe my dad was okay and Mom and Dominique had gone home.

The lobby was quiet and one guard was on duty. He asked if he could help us. I gave him my name and requested to see my father. The man just looked at me and said that I couldn't do that.

I repeated, "I want to see my dad. I didn't drive five hours for nothing."

In an unemotional voice the guard said, "Well, you didn't drive it for nothing. Your dad passed away." As I listened to his words, a wave of heat rushed from my toes to my brain. I felt hot and dizzy but I knew I wouldn't faint. The light-headedness had come from a sudden feeling of anger.

I turned around to face Lloyd and then, with the front of my forearm, I slammed him in the chest and began to sob uncontrollably. Lloyd took me in his arms and tried to comfort me. But nothing could ease the pain I felt.

Lloyd

I couldn't believe it when I heard the guard tell Isabelle that her father had died. Just like that. He had no sympathy in his voice . . . no tact. If it had been under any other circumstances, I probably would have punched him right in the mouth.

When Isabelle turned to me, I thought she was going to die right then and there. I put my arms out and pulled her close. She began to cry the way I have never seen anyone cry before or since. I hugged and held her and she had a hard time even walking. She just didn't want to let go. It was heart-wrenching to watch her go through this hell and not be able to do anything about it.

Isabelle

Lloyd took me home, and as soon as I got through the door, I jumped into my family's arms and they realized that I knew what had happened. I discovered that, when I had spoken to Josée earlier, my mom and brother had been right beside her, but because they were crying so much, they couldn't speak to me. Josée hadn't thought it appropriate to give me such news over the telephone but she told Dominique and my mom that she sensed that I knew.

The day had been so difficult for them. Apparently, my dad left work early in the afternoon. He always liked to cook and since Dominique and Josée were coming over, he had offered to prepare dinner. Dad had put everything in the oven and set the table by the time my mom came home. He told her that dinner would be ready in a half hour and in the meantime he was going for his daily walk. My dad never returned home.

A man and his little boy were driving down the street when the boy spotted my father lying on the sidewalk. He died three houses away from home. The doctors weren't sure what happened. They said he had arrhythmia and water in the lungs, which happens when your heart hasn't been beating normally for a while.

After I arrived home, we stayed up for the rest of the night, just talking. The table was still set for dinner and remained that way for a long time. We couldn't even throw out the meat Dad had cooked. I finally went to bed with my mom in her and Dad's room while Dominique and Josée stayed in the guest room. But it was sad to hear my mother. She cried so much and then hugged Dad's pillow and even kissed his shoes. That was the hardest part . . . seeing my mom like that.

I couldn't sleep so I got up and wandered around the house, looking for pictures of my father. Then I saw his jewellery on a table—his engineering ring, his wedding ring and other pieces. I picked up each one and put them on. His engineering ring fit my index finger perfectly.

The next day, I asked my mother if I could have the ring. She said yes and I have never taken it off, not even for an hour. In fact, it is the only ring that Lloyd lets me wear when we skate, since it is dangerous to wear any jewellery on your hands. That ring is probably worth about only five dollars and it really is ugly, but it is priceless to me. It means my dad is with me—always.

Lloyd

The wake lasted three days and I spent from morning until night with Isabelle. I believed it was my job to be there for her. No matter what she or her family needed, I would take care of it.

I remember the day of the funeral. It was so emotional. Isabelle got up and spoke about her father at the church, which I thought took a great deal of courage. I mean, I don't know if I could do the same if it had been my dad. She spoke very well and I was extremely proud of her.

At the cemetery, I watched Isabelle as she placed roses on Gill's coffin. Both she and her Dad loved roses. Everyone left to go back to Claudette's place but Isabelle and I remained behind. We stood by her dad's grave for another thirty minutes by ourselves and she asked me questions that I couldn't answer.

"Why couldn't I have been at home?" she wondered, and I think it was at that point that Isabelle realized how much she was away because shortly thereafter she hated being on the road. I think she began to believe that every time she went away something bad was going to happen.

Isabelle

I have to say that, when my dad passed away, Lloyd and my girl-friend, Julie, were there for me every single minute. She and Lloyd would sit quietly, and I knew if I needed anything, they were there for me.

Jean-Luc helped me, too, but in a different way. He and my dad had met only a few times so obviously he wasn't as sad as we were. I remember one day when Jean-Luc was over he took out the vacuum cleaner, informing us that he was going to clean the house. We were all just sitting around, feeling very down. Jean-Luc came in the room, wearing an apron and with a bandanna around his head. He didn't say a word but began to dust around us with a serious look on his face. We all stared at him and, one by one, started to laugh. He was just trying to put some lightness into our lives. The next day, I went to put on my shoes and discovered someone had filled one with shaving cream. That someone was obviously Jean-Luc, who was attempting to say in his own way that life goes on and that laughter is an important part of healing.

While Jean-Luc tried to lift my spirits, Lloyd, who had been closer to my dad, was trying to deal with his own grief as well as mine. My best friend must have spent eighteen hours a day at the house, only going home to sleep. But that's the kind of person Lloyd is and I know how much my dad would have appreciated his thoughtfulness.

For a long time, Dad and Lloyd didn't get along but only because they were very similar. They were both stubborn people who always had to be right. About six months before my father passed away, someone commented that Lloyd was cold and unfriendly with people. Dad heard this and immediately came to Lloyd's defense. He said, "You feel that way only because you don't know him. He is a great guy, and for the people he loves, he will do anything to take care of them. As long as I know that he is going to be around my daughter, I have no doubt that she will be safe and that someone is there to look after her."

This is so true. If a person says something negative about me, Lloyd will take offense. If I am lost, he comes to get me. We could be 10,000 miles apart but if he knew I needed him, he would drop everything for me, as I would for him. When I had a car accident, Lloyd was the first person I called. He took care of both me and my car and all the details as well. I know my dad believed that I would be protected as long as Lloyd was with me.

Lloyd

In the end, Gill and I had great respect for each other. Initially, I think he was afraid when Isabelle and I began skating together. I was much bigger than she was and had a reputation for saying things that weren't acceptable in our sport.

But, as time went on, I believe he realized that, no matter what, if Isabelle and I were together, nothing bad would ever happen to his little girl. He knew that I was always going to be there for her, even if he couldn't be, and as long as I was near Isabelle, she would be safe.

Isabelle

Everything came to a stop for a while. I knew I wanted to skate again. That was what my dad would have wanted and I realized how important it was to me, but for the first few weeks I just couldn't concentrate.

Two weeks after he passed away, we were scheduled to compete in Japan for the NHK Trophy. The only reason I agreed to go was that I was thinking, I have to keep living right now and the only thing that will keep me going is my skating. It gave me something to do to take my mind off things. It wasn't easy, though, because I just didn't feel like being at the rink.

We skated very poorly in Japan. Lloyd fell in the short program and we didn't do much better in the long. We came fourth overall and I couldn't wait to get home to my family and friends. Because of my dad, I had suddenly realized that these people were not going to be around forever and I wanted to spend as much time as possible with them while I could.

My outlook was quite harsh for a while. When we didn't skate well in Japan, I really didn't care. I thought, We are all going to die anyway. What did it really matter, what we did in life? I was very depressed and couldn't seem to find my way out.

Dr. Jensen came and talked to me and then he spoke with Lloyd and our coaches because they were having a hard time coping with my emotions. We all sat down and talked and eventually, through individual and group sessions, we learned how to deal with it as a team.

Lloyd

We tried to skate but for the next little while Isabelle wasn't there emotionally. She didn't care about skating. She had just lost her father, who had been instrumental in introducing her to the sport, and she wanted him there.

Some days we would skate for five minutes and other days we would manage a whole session, but every practice seemed to end in tears. If something didn't go well, Isabelle just didn't care. She didn't want to be there.

Josée believed that it was best for Isabelle to keep skating and that training would take her mind off what had happened. However, Isabelle had no desire to be at the rink. She wanted to be at home with her mom and brother.

We all began to work with Dr. Jensen to learn how to deal with what Isabelle was going through. As we talked, I began to realize what Isabelle needed from day to day and, with his help, things slowly started to repair themselves. I learned, in particular, how to work without being so critical at this very fragile time in Isabelle's life. As a team, we learned to commit our practice schedules to paper so there would be no discussions or arguments about what had to be done on a daily basis.

In the meantime, Christmas was fast approaching and we again were doing the "Ice Capades." Although we weren't skating every day, we began to spend a lot more time together. I think Isabelle found it comforting for me to be around.

The Brasseurs didn't celebrate Christmas that year and I recall Isabelle giving out presents she had bought for Christmas months later. I was with them but it wasn't a happy time and it was difficult for Isabelle not to have her father there over the holidays.

Isabelle

I can't recall many details about Christmas that year but do remember feeling so lonely for my dad. We did the "Ice Capades" at the Forum again and I spent many hours discussing my feelings with Lloyd.

Once the therapy sessions with Dr. Jensen were over, I found that I was skating for different reasons. I started going to the rink to see Lloyd, Josée and Eric—people I loved and had fun with. I still cared about skating and worked hard, but now, if I wasn't skating well, it wasn't the end of the world for me. Instead, I just appreciated each and every minute I was spending with my favorite people. At the end of a day, I would thank Lloyd for being my friend and tell him what a great time I'd had. I would then turn to Josée and say, "Today was fun. Now, I'm going home to see my mom." Being with the people I loved and telling them how I felt was all I cared about.

I developed a peace within myself that I had never experienced before. It lasted only a few months and how I wish I could find that same peacefulness again. I think about it now and wonder where it came from. Perhaps it was there because I was staying with my mom. I had moved back home and we relied heavily on each other. I found myself looking after her, and by the very fact that she was with me, I knew I would be okay as well. We gained much of our strength from each other and she gave me the love that only a mother can give to her child.

Whether that peace developed from being with my mom or came as a special gift from my dad, I'm not sure. Maybe it was a combination of the two. But whatever its source, I was grateful for the strength and insight it gave me.

Lloyd

While we were performing in the "Ice Capades," we spent as much as twelve hours a day at the rink and Isabelle and I had a chance to really connect again. We began to talk about skating and life and how we viewed our roles in sport and in the world. Suddenly, we were able to see the big picture again and everything fell into perspective.

In the past, if one of us had fallen while skating, we would get so upset. Now, we began to realize that skating wasn't the be all and end all. If we fell or missed something, or even came last at a competition, the sun would still rise in the morning.

From that point on, I began to change my own philosophy. Skating is just skating. It would be here tomorrow and there were far more important things in life such as family and friends.

Over the next month, Isabelle and I both took a much lighter view of what we did and began to enjoy ourselves on the ice again. We realized that we had taken skating far too seriously in the past and had somehow lost sight of what we were in it for.

By the time of the 1993 Nationals, Isabelle had developed a tranquillity that I hadn't seen in her before. I, too, was experiencing an element of calmness that, although unfamiliar, felt good. As for the upcoming competition, I don't know if we were prepared as a team; there had been so many changes in our professional and personal lives. The one thing I did know was that we were definitely ready as individuals.

CHAPTER EIGHT

Skating in Harmony

Lloyd

THE CANADIAN CHAMPIONSHIPS in Hamilton, Ontario, would set the stage for our new look. Because we hadn't performed much between November and February, we would be under the scrutiny of both the public and media. After my initial trepidation, I was now at last becoming more comfortable with the program and actually enjoyed doing it.

So much had occurred before Nationals that my memories of the competition are now a blur. However, I distinctly remember the mostly positive comments regarding our programs and the flurry of interviews that our presence caused. Everybody wanted to speak with us about the death of Isabelle's father but we directed all requests to Josée, who advised us on which interview to do. At that point, it was Isabelle's call as to whether or not we would accommodate the press. I wasn't making any decisions with regards to interviews.

We skated strongly in both programs and everybody wanted to know what had motivated the change. The majority of people seemed impressed but some said Isabelle and I were copying the

Russians. We didn't agree. Yes, our style had been modified but it was still our own. It was just more refined and polished.

Isabelle

I was at ease going into the 1993 Nationals and knew that if we skated well, there was a good chance we could win again. Tuffy and Doug had since turned professional and everyone looked to us to take our fourth Canadian title.

When we arrived, everybody was so sympathetic and supportive to us. That helped a lot.

It was strange, but I felt as if my father was with me the whole time. At the beginning of our program, I quietly said, "Dad, just sit down, relax and enjoy it," and I truly believed that is just what he did. It was difficult for my mom, though. I had started taking her everywhere with me that I could, not wanting to be apart. She sat by herself in the stands, where he had always been by her side. Mom just wasn't used to being alone.

Although we were happy when we won, there wasn't the usual excitement between Lloyd and me . . . just a composed and thankful acceptance.

Lloyd

Jean-Michel Bombardier and his partner, Michelle Menzies, had also qualified for Worlds that year and Isabelle and I found it fun and more relaxing to be able to practice with another team. Although it was always tough to train between Nationals and Worlds, this time our attention was centered on how we were feeling rather than on criticizing our programs or each other. We were just getting the work done and then moving on.

Another simulation was organized at Maple Leaf Gardens in Toronto, where we could have chosen to perform either the long or the short program. My vote was for the short. Call me lazy but I didn't want to do the long because it was just too lengthy and difficult. But Isabelle preferred to practice it and Josée absolutely insisted. So the long we did. All the people from the association were there as well as other skaters, coaches, judges and sports psychologists. We only had a short warm-up but Isabelle and I skated perfectly and were again encouraged by the favorable comments.

There was more publicity than usual going into 1993 Worlds. It was to be held at the same rink in Prague, Czechoslovakia, where Donald Jackson had won the men's title and Maria and Otto Jelinek had taken the pairs championship in 1962. Prague was considered to be *the* place where Canadians had great success in the past and people were looking to us and Kurt Browning to continue the tradition.

Our practices were well organized because we now trained by doing complete run-throughs. Isabelle and I were skating flawlessly and, before we knew it, our practice sessions were packed with spectators. Each day led to the next without any turmoil or arguments. In fact, the week seemed to fly by—it all seemed so easy. We were just so in tune with our programs and with each other.

We drew a good position to skate in the short program but it didn't really matter to us. Isabelle and I knew the elements we had to perform. All we had to do was go out and skate well.

As our names were called, Isabelle caught my eye and said, "Let's enjoy ourselves," and that is exactly what we did. We skated just as we had at practice and I remember thinking at the end of the program that it had been effortless—and that it should always be that way.

We were first after the short and normally would have been extremely hyped after skating so well. Although I was excited, I wasn't as keyed-up as usual and Isabelle remained very matter-of-fact about it all.

Isabelle

In the past, before I competed, I had a habit of arriving at the rink an hour and a half before we were scheduled to skate. I would then literally run all over the arena, trying to locate my parents. When I spotted them in the stands, I would climb up, give them a kiss and then return to ice level. On the day of the long program, someone pointed out my mom to me as soon as I walked in, which saved me the time of looking for her.

I had been so happy that she'd been able to make it to Worlds. My mother hadn't wanted to travel alone and had looked for someone to accompany her. Mondor, a sponsor of ours, heard about the situation and Mrs. Deslauriers, the owner of the company, offered to go with my mom. Mondor also paid for part of her trip.

When I reached my mother in the stands, she gave me a kiss and then whispered, "You are such a big girl now. You can do it and now you have a helper up there. Just don't worry." She then opened her hand and said, "See what I have with me?" In her palm lay my father's wedding ring. We looked at each other and smiled and I knew that both my parents would be there while I skated.

Josée, Uschi and Eric were all at Worlds and it was especially nice to have Eric with us. Before we went on to perform the long program, Josée took my hand and said in a very serious voice, "Do you remember all those times that your dad told you he wished he could skate for you and land the jumps, so you wouldn't have to worry about them? Well, now he is going to be on the ice with you. He's going to pull you up by your hair and hold on. He won't let you fall. Believe in yourself."

My coach was reinforcing what I already believed to be true. There was no doubt in my mind that Dad would be watching from a front row seat.

Lloyd

I couldn't afford to bring both my parents to Prague and, as it turned out, my mother wasn't enthusiastic about making the long journey anyway. She's not crazy about flying and so it was decided that only my dad would go.

It was good for me to have him at Worlds. We would meet for lunch and then go our separate ways, with never any pressure from him to spend more time with me than my schedule would allow.

Everyone knew and liked my father, as he is such a comfortable person to be around. He is genuine and honest, and his support always gave me strength at competitions.

The day of the long program, I thought a lot about whether this was going to be the year that we would be able to go out and put it all together. During our practice we'd had a small, ten-minute stretch where Isabelle seemed to lose her focus. We couldn't do anything and she began to get upset. But after speaking to Josée and Eric, all of a sudden everything returned to normal. We had been skating the program without a hitch all week and, really, there was no reason to worry about it. As long as we were able to nail down the first part, we both knew we would be fine.

Right off the bat, we had double Axels . . . no problem. We then came around and performed our triple lateral. At that point, it felt as if we were riding the crest of a huge wave. We had only one difficult element left, the throw triple toe, which we executed perfectly. As we continued to skate, I was supposed to be looking at Isabelle, but out of the corner of my eye I noticed the whole Canadian team, along with my father and Isabelle's mother, jumping up and down in excitement. They were on an elevated stage area with the television cameras and were highly visible. I forced my mind back to the program, as we still had another lift and jump combination. By the time of our final element, which was a death spiral, I couldn't hear the music above the standing ovation from our large group of Canadian fans. I thought, This is it. We've done it. We've won!

Isabelle

When we finished, Lloyd knelt down on one knee and kissed my hand. With tears in his eyes, he said, "Gill, this one was for you."

We skated off, received our marks and found that we had been given first place by all the judges. My mom, Lloyd's dad, our coaches and most of the Canadian team were crying. Josée said, "I can't believe it. My little girl is finally world champion."

I looked at all the people who I loved so dearly, and as I realized my dad's face wasn't among them, I began to weep uncontrollably. Although I believed he was with me in spirit, I sorely missed his physical presence. I sobbed, "All he wanted was to see me skate the way I did tonight. Now I am world champion and he is not here to share it with me."

Everyone gathered around me and said, "But he *was* there. He was helping you all the way, holding you up. Your dad was the first one to see everything and knew you were going to win before we did. He had the best seat in the house!"

Josée told me that, just before our second throw, she had looked up and said, "*Now* help her! Now it is time!" and had continued speaking to my father all the way through our program. When I heard that everyone really believed my dad was there, I suddenly felt very lucky. Not only had Lloyd and I accomplished our dream, but I also deeply appreciated the fact that I had such wonderful, sensitive people in my life.

Lloyd

We had been on the podium before, but to stand at the top as world champions was a terrific feeling. As we received our gold medals and heard the Canadian national anthem being played, it was more satisfying than emotional for me. Finally, all the time, effort and work had paid off. We had gotten the job done.

When it was all over, my partner and I were ready to go on tour through Europe and have some fun. The Canadian contingent was small, consisting of only Isabelle, me and Karen Preston. Kurt, who had also won in Prague, had bowed out of the three-week tour. But we had a great time skiing and taking in the sights with Yuka Sato and Mark Mitchell.

This ISU tour, like the others, was not extravagant by any means; we played small venues and stayed in tiny hotels. Nine-hour bus rides took up much of the time and our muscles grew from lugging our own bags everywhere. But Isabelle and I were on such a high after our triumph at Worlds that nothing seemed to matter. We laughed at everything and delighted in performing at each of the fifteen cities on the tour.

Brussels was the exception, though. It just wasn't my day. First I got kicked in the leg during practice. It was sore but no big deal. Later that night, we were halfway through our second number when Isabelle came down from a triple twist and elbowed me in the eye. The next thing I knew, there was blood all over my face and on the ice.

Isabelle

Lloyd and I were in practice when I accidentally kicked him in the leg and gave him a charley horse. When we performed that night, his leg was causing some pain and I thought maybe we should cancel the second number. But Lloyd insisted that he was okay. In the middle of our routine, he threw me in the air for the triple twist, but because his leg was stiff, he didn't quite throw me high enough. When I landed, my arms weren't in the right position and I hit him in the eye.

I was skating backwards and couldn't see Lloyd. Then I heard him say, "Don't look but I'm bleeding here. Just keep going, though. I'm fine."

When I turned around, I gasped as I saw blood running down half his face. I was upset but he insisted that it was only a little cut. At the end of the program, we were doing a Detroiter, where Lloyd holds me over his head while I lie in a horizontal position. He began to spin faster and faster until a circle of blood formed around us as it flew off his face. It was so gross but somehow we managed to finish the number.

Lloyd

The cut appeared much worse than it was and only took five stitches to close. My eye quickly began to turn black and over dinner that night I took a lot of kidding as everyone joked about Isabelle belting me.

The tour finished uneventfully and we headed home to a rather emotional reception at the airport in Montreal. My mother and father had driven down and joined Isabelle's family to greet us. It was particularly nice to see my mom because she hadn't been at Worlds and was so excited about our win. Josée, Eric and all our friends from the rink were also there with posters and flowers. Because almost a month had passed since Prague, Isabelle and I had almost forgotten that we were world champions. But seeing and talking to everyone allowed us to relive the experience.

There were many requests for interviews and appearances and we couldn't believe the mail that poured in. It seemed that it just wasn't Quebec that was proud, but the entire country. In fact, the warmth that fellow Canadians expressed to Isabelle and me was so intense that it tended to help us forget many of the struggles we had been through in order to get where we were. It was nice to know how much people cared.

Isabelle

We had about a week off before we were to join the Tom Collins tour and I took advantage of it to rest up. Although Jean-Luc and I were still together, we hadn't been able to see much of each other because we were competing at the same time and had actually both won Worlds that year.

I had last seen him in Prague when he was on the World Cup circuit. He had somehow managed to arrange a couple of days off and had taken the train to meet me in Czechoslovakia. Apparently, he had quite an adventure getting there as he didn't have his visa and wound up at a police station along the way. Jean-Luc had to leave before Lloyd and I competed since his event was held within twenty-four hours of mine in Austria. Because no phone calls were going through between the two countries, the only way we found out that the other had won was through the media. It took us two weeks to finally hook up with each other by telephone.

Lloyd

Once home from the tour, Isabelle and I took our usual sabbaticals and then were back on the ice, facing a decision about which long program we should do for the coming Olympic year. There had been some thought about keeping the same one because it had been received so well.

In the past, Isabelle and I had always maintained a strict policy not to repeat a program back to back. It was too repetitive for us and we believed that if people saw the same thing over again, they might have been bored. But everyone was urging us to the contrary, and although we weren't entirely comfortable, it did seem the logical way to go. A few minor revisions were made along with a complete change of costume, and once the decision had been made, Isabelle and I settled into perfecting the program.

Isabelle

It was a calm summer for me. Since the death of my father, everything was easy. Although the peace I had discovered over the past few months ebbed away by then, I was still in a very different frame of mind. Nothing was a big deal to me, no matter what the issue.

The lease on my apartment expired in July, and since I had moved back home with my mother, I decided to let it go for good. I enjoyed living with my mom and I know she was happy with our arrangement as well.

Once Lloyd and I made the decision to repeat our long program with a few changes, we began work on the short program, which was skated to the "Beer Barrel Polka." Although we liked it, we found it couldn't be developed past a certain stage. It just didn't grow.

In October, we flew to Norway for the Pireutten competition, which was held at the same rink that the Olympics would be staged at. It was a good opportunity for us to try out the programs and get a feel for the venue.

Lloyd

The reason we had opted to perform at Pireutten was to prepare ourselves for the Olympic Games. By participating in this event, we would have seen everything and would know exactly what to expect when we arrived in February.

We skated very well in the competition and came second behind Dmitriev and Mishkutenok but word filtered back to us from the judges about our short program. To many of them, it wasn't classy enough or up to the caliber they expected. Some of these judges were going to be at the Olympics and Worlds and Isabelle and I knew we couldn't ignore their comments.

Our next competition was *Trophée Lalique* but we pulled out and asked if we could compete in Japan at a later date instead. We had decided to change the short program and needed time to create another one. We needn't have worried, though. Our new program fell together in a few days, as if it was meant to be. The music was far more dramatic and powerful, with a gypsy theme, and it immediately felt right to us.

Divisionals were held in Sherbrooke, Quebec, that year and, with the CFSA's go-ahead, we competed only in the seniors pair short program. Frances Dafoe, who had again designed our costumes, was going to be a judge at that event and we wanted her opinion on our new program. Changing it was apparently the right decision because Frances and the other judges rated it far superior.

The next day, we left to compete in the NHK Trophy. Only Uschi accompanied us, since our coaches were in the middle of Divisionals. It was very relaxing to be with her because not only is Uschi a great choreographer but she is also an excellent motivator. Her laid-back approach encourages an easygoing attitude from those around her.

We won the prestigious Japanese competition, which was something we had always strived for, and then returned home to perform in the five-day show over Christmas. By then, Isabelle and I were very comfortable with both programs. We knew exactly what we were doing in each one and the familiarity of the long, in particular, gave us the extra confidence we would need in the coming months.

Isabelle

While in Japan, a few of us went out to dinner one night. I was walking down the street, talking to Karen Preston and not really paying attention to where I was going, when I walked into a post. I must have hit it pretty hard because for a moment I didn't know what had happened, and it was only when I saw stars that I realized what I'd done.

The accident didn't bother me until I returned home and began skating in the shows at the Forum. During the triple twist, I started to experience a type of whiplash; a burning sensation ran down my back whenever I turned too quickly. I couldn't move half my body for at least twenty seconds after that and decided I'd better seek treatment immediately.

It seems one of the vertebrae in my neck was out of place but we couldn't figure out how I had done it. Two weeks later, I was speaking to Uschi and told her about the trouble I was having. She commented that I had probably injured my neck when I walked into the post. It turned out that she was correct but until then I had never connected the two incidents.

Prior to 1994 Nationals, we didn't rehearse any twists because I couldn't turn my head. I knew the short program wouldn't be a problem but I was worried what would happen when we did the triple twist in the long. We advised the judges of my injury and they agreed that if I experienced the burning sensation and immobility while skating, we could stop our program for the time it took me to recover.

These Nationals were to be our last, and although I was feeling a little emotional, I wasn't sad. In a way, I was happy that my amateur days were almost over. I had accomplished what I'd wanted to and was looking forward to the future. I only wanted to skate well and cherish each and every moment.

Just before we went on the ice to compete in the short program, Josée began to cry. I guess she was experiencing some nostalgia for all that we had been through together but I didn't let it bother me. My focus now was on the job to be done.

While out in the warm-up, Lloyd and I had received an ovation from the spectators, and when they called our names to do the program, people were standing and clapping before we even began. I think it was the audience's way of saying goodbye and I felt so thankful for the support they had shown us over the years.

My neck and back didn't give me a problem during the program and we couldn't have skated any better, yet we came off to receive marks of 5.8 and 5.9. I remember commenting to my brother that the only thing missing in our career was a 6.0 at Nationals and that it was too bad it was something we would never see. Dominique replied, "Don't worry, you may still have a chance to get one tomorrow."

I looked at him skeptically and said, "In the long program? I doubt it."

Lloyd

Before the long program, Josée, Eric, Uschi, Isabelle and I were talking backstage about this being our last Canadian championships when the reality suddenly hit me. This was it. It was my seventeenth time at the Nationals, which was the record for any figure skater in Canada, and now it was all ending.

Just before we stepped onto the ice, Josée said to us, "Skate well for me one last time." We came out in our purple outfits and again the crowd stood up before we even began. It felt so good to know that people were behind us.

We skated perfectly, and about two-thirds of the way into the program, the audience started to clap and didn't stop until it was well over. We had been a little nervous about Isabelle's injury during the triple twist but she appeared to be okay and we continued the program without a flaw.

As we took our bows, flowers rained out of the stands. Normally skaters are supposed to be off the ice when the marks are given, but Isabelle and I stayed out longer than usual to try to pick everything up. While still on the ice, I heard the first of the marks being announced for technical merit—6.0! Isabelle and I rushed off to hug Josée and listen in wonderment as a few more 6.0's went up. It was fantastic.

The crowd was going wild, there were still flowers on the ice and all the reporters were trying to get interviews at the same time. Kris Wirtz, who was performing behind us, came over and said, "Thanks a lot. I sure feel like skating now."

I answered, "Hey, there are good vibes out there. Use them." Kris and his partner, Kristy Sargeant, then skated the best they had since the last Olympics and ended up in second place. After that, Kris said he hoped to skate after us all the time. Jason Turner and Jamie Salé came third to make up the rest of the Olympic team, and although we were happy for them, we felt sorry for Josée because her other pairs teams hadn't made it. It was especially devastating for Jean-Michel and Michelle, who had had a bit of a rough year. We had all thought they could pull it together but it just didn't happen and it wasn't easy to see them crying backstage.

But, from our standpoint, we had ended on the highest possible note, and when we received our medals I was a little teary eyed, knowing that this was it. Our Nationals was over. We would never be back again. I think I was feeling it more than Isabelle because I had been around so long. In all those years through the novice, junior and senior levels, I had always made it to the podium and I was really going to miss it because I loved competing. I was also apprehensive about the future. After the season was over, we would be stepping into a new way of life and the thought of that was a little scary.

Isabelle

At Nationals, I was presented with the Dennis Coi Award, to my complete surprise. The award is given annually to the figure skater who "keeps skating and life in perspective" and I was extremely honored to receive it.

I was also relieved that Nationals were done and I wasn't really thinking about my future beyond the Olympics and Worlds. I still wasn't sure what I was going to do when my amateur career was over and, for the time being, turned all my attention to the upcoming Games.

We had learned from our experience in 1992 how to deal with the pressure and were very cautious about giving interviews prior to the Olympics. I didn't speak with anyone unless it was well planned. My mom answered the telephone at home and was instructed to tell people I wasn't in unless it was Lloyd or a close friend. If the media called, my brother would find out what they wanted and then speak to us. If we decided against the interview, Dominique would inform the reporter. In this way, I was shielded from the outside world and didn't have the added stress of turning down requests. Josée and Eric also spoke to many people for us as they worked together to try to make things easier for Lloyd and me. During this period, I also avoided going anywhere in public. Jean-Luc was in the same situation we were and so the two of us basically kept a low profile and tended to stay home most of the time.

Lloyd

The big talk of the day seemed to be how we felt about having to compete against the professionals at the Olympics who had been allowed by the ISU to reinstate. Having them back was going to affect us—no question—but what really bothered me was the impact of the ruling on the people below us in ranking. Some of these athletes might have been competing for ten or twelve years. The main goal in their skating career was to make the Olympic team. Then the International Skating Union reinstated the professionals and there was no way any country was not going to select the pro over the amateur to represent it. As I've said before, the sport is too political. This decision took the spot away from someone else who had worked years to qualify for the Olympic team, and both Isabelle and I strongly felt that the judgment made by the ISU was a big mistake.

I think the regulation came about due to greed on the part of the athletes. Skating happens to be at the peak of its popularity. The more times you are seen on television, the more your name is out there and that leads to dollars and cents, if you're successful. I don't begrudge anyone that and I don't harbor any ill feelings about it. I just didn't really believe that most of the professionals were returning for the love of the sport, as they would have liked us to believe. In my opinion, their thinking was more, "I'm coming back because there is a lot of money to be made in the future if I can do well at the Olympics now."

As I've stated, I don't hold anything against any of these athletes, only the bureaucracy for making the rule in the first place. That is what Isabelle and I had been most vocal about and what we had been arguing against. Our feelings had nothing to do with who the athletes were or how much talent they had. These skaters were our friends. But, right or wrong, the decision had been made and the consequences would remain to be seen.

Isabelle

Lloyd had already objected when the announcement to reinstate the professionals was made the previous autumn and some people concluded he had been a little too vocal. But I think that a person should say what's on their mind and all Lloyd was doing was expressing an honest opinion.

I, too, believed the judgment made by the ISU was wrong, but at the same time I knew there was nothing I could do about the situation. Even if I complained, it would not be changed.

As the competition drew nearer, Lloyd told me that he thought I should be dealing with the press on that topic from now on. He had made his feelings quite clear in the past and believed it would be better for us if he just focused on his job at hand. I had no problem with that and basically told the media that we didn't hold anything against the professional skaters, only the rule that had allowed them to return. I also said that Lloyd and I were just going to do our best in Lillehammer and live with the fact that the professionals would be there.

Lloyd

I was still bitter about the subject prior to leaving for Norway and so I asked Isabelle to deal with the press on that issue. She was able to get our point across more gently than I would have and I, in turn, was able to concentrate on skating.

We still had three weeks of training left and found it tough getting back into the grind of practicing the programs. Isabelle and I were the only team at the rink and were beginning to feel the isolation as we tried to focus on our skating. We had been ready since Nationals to compete, and as each day passed, I grew more impatient to just go and get it over with.

Isabelle

Everything was going according to schedule, and although training was difficult, we managed to maintain a calm attitude. In my mind, nothing could be worse than what we had been through in 1992, and if for some reason we didn't do well at these Olympics, then at least we would know how to deal and live with it. I believed we had grown that much individually and as a team.

Two days before we left, we were practicing the triple lateral when my ribs were hit really hard. I couldn't breathe or move but refused to have X rays. I suspected they were cracked but didn't want to find out for sure. It was better for me mentally not to know as I didn't want any negativity affecting our performance. Skating in our last Olympics was far too meaningful to us and I was resolved to let nothing stand in the way of our goal.

CHAPTER NINE

All That Glitters

Isabelle

ASIDE from the rib, we were prepared both physically and mentally. In 1992, at the Olympics in Albertville, we had been ready physically but we got nervous and stressed out. We worked hard in 1993 and 1994 to overcome the tension and didn't want to put ourselves under that kind of pressure again. We had decided we would just go out onto the ice and do what we do every day because every day out there is pretty good.

Even though we were the best of the amateurs, I knew our chances of winning the gold medal were slim but I thought we could take the silver or bronze. Yet we realized that even for a bronze we had to give the best we had. Just one mistake could put us in fourth or fifth position.

We arrived in Norway seven days prior to our competition, which was to be held on the second day of the Olympics. Our first stop was Oslo where we took part in one seminar after another. There, we met the team physician, learned who was in charge of security and found out who would be looking after us while we were at the games. We received our uniforms but not without mishap.

Because the sizes had been requested two years in advance, by the time we actually got to Norway nothing fit! It was a hectic schedule but somehow everything fell into place and we were finally on our way to Hamar.

Lloyd

Situated 45 km south of Lillehammer, Hamar is the small town that housed the Olympic Amphitheater. This was to be the venue for the figure skating and short track speedskating competitions. The pairs teams, consisting of Kris Wirtz and Kristy Sargeant, Jason Turner and Jamie Salé and Isabelle and myself, arrived a few days ahead of the rest of the Canadian team.

Security was always a priority at the Olympics and these Games were no different. At the village entrance the bus went through one check and then, after everyone got off, we went through another. The entire complex was fenced in and you could virtually live inside, leaving only to go to your venue. There was a library, post office, gift store, little food store and the dormitories, which were set up in university style.

The Canadian figure skating team has a reputation for being the one with the most spirit, and so right away we set about decorating the dorm with Canadian flags, banners and faxes we had received. Everyone had their name and an envelope on their door so we could leave messages for each other. There was a team room at the end of the hall that belonged to our team leaders, but it was open to any of us day or night. We stocked the room with food that we had collected from the Canadian Olympic Association. We also made sure we had a little wine and beer in the fridge. You are not supposed to drink in the dorms but everyone does. That room quickly became our own special haven. If your roommate was sleeping or if you wanted the company of others, you went to the team room. Our quarters were right above the cafeteria, so we were lucky. We never had to go outside, which was nice considering the temperature was hovering at 30° below. Norway is a beautiful country and with all the snow we felt right at home. We loved it but I think some of the other skaters from the milder climates, such as South Africa, might have had some problems adjusting to the frigid temperatures.

There were a lot fewer people in Hamar than in Lillehammer and very few places to go. When we were able to make it into town for a pizza or a beer, we would often see the same people over and over again. I think they were overwhelmed that the Olympics were being held in their country, and they showed us right from the very beginning that they were going to do everything in their power to make us feel at home. They were extremely supportive of the Olympics and very much behind their own athletes.

Wherever we went, we always tried to wear something that showed we were from Canada to spark people's interest. It was fun trading pins, buying postcards and talking to people to find out where they were from and why they were there.

Besides the pairs couples, the Canadian skating team consisted of Kurt Browning, Elvis Stojko, Sébastien Britten, Josée Chouinard, Susan Humphreys, Shae-Lynn Bourne and Victor Kraatz. Kurt was the world team captain and I was the national captain. Between the two of us, we tried to help the others whenever possible. If the younger, more inexperienced athletes had any questions about how to dress for a certain function or how to deal with an unfamiliar situation, Kurt and I were there to provide answers.

Over the years, we have worked hard to maintain a great support system for each other—this team spirit probably began in 1981 with Rob McCall, Tracy Wilson and Brian Orser. Back then, we tried to develop a spirit of unity and camaraderie, and it has just kept getting stronger. It's a great feeling to know the team is fully behind you when you are out there on the ice.

Isabelle

Upon arriving in Hamar, we settled into the dormitory. Josée Chouinard, who would be getting there just before the opening ceremony, was to be my roommate again. When you are at a competition like the Olympics, it is very important to room with someone you are compatible with and Josée and I always got along well. Stress runs high at these events, and it helps to know your roommate well enough to pick up on her moods.

I was also happy to hear that all of the speedskating was to be in Hamar. The short track is always held at the same venue as the figure skating, but this year I would be able to take in much of the long track as well, which was to take place at the Olympic Hall, also situated in the town.

When I awoke the next morning, I looked out and saw that it had snowed during the night. Everything looked like a picture postcard—peaceful, white and beautiful. In a way, I was glad our venue was not in Lillehammer, which would be overflowing with people. Because only the figure skaters and speedskaters were in our village, it felt like a much smaller competition. At the Olympics, many athletes get nervous because the media and spectators are so overwhelming. But the quiet of our little village certainly helped my nerves.

Lloyd

The Olympic Amphitheater was a fantastic arena and I was impressed with its facilities. There was ample room to warm up, which is a luxury at a large event like the Olympics where television cameras and crews jostle each other trying to get their stories. The rink's dimensions and ice thickness conformed to Olympic standards and we found the ice to be very good.

Each practice session was forty-five minutes to an hour long, twice a day. Everything was organized by Josée and Eric. Because we were favoured to win a medal at the games, we had a lot of media attention at the practices, which we always shared with the Australian and Chinese skaters.

It was Canada versus Russia and amateur versus professional, so many spectators filled the stands. We enjoyed the crowds because we find it easier to skate when there is an audience. Because of this attention, we planned every little detail of the practice ahead, right down to what we would wear. Our outfits always matched and really looked good. We knew exactly what we were going to do when we got onto the ice, so we never appeared disorganized.

All the judges had to be there as well to learn the programs and familiarize themselves with new elements. As usual, the East judges huddled together, as did the judges from the West. And certain judges and coaches would be in conversation with each other. Judging is supposed to be straightforward but we all know it is biased. Isabelle and I try not to let it bother us since there isn't much we can do about it.

Instead of worrying about the upcoming competition, we were concentrating on what we could leave out of practice to alleviate Isabelle's pain. We were also trying to take some pressure off the lifts because the force of my throwing and catching Isabelle on her injured rib was tremendous.

We didn't worry about doing well every day; we had some great practices and some not so great. There was no question that the injury was a hurdle we had to overcome. Because, at the Games, the athletes are under the guidance of the IOC drug laws, Isabelle couldn't take any pills for the pain. We just had to work through it.

Isabelle

I had trouble dealing with the brightness of the rink. Because of the lights on the ceiling, the silver seats and the shiny ice, everything appeared to be white.

Before I jump, I always look down on the ice, and at this arena I could see the reflection of the lights. During the first practice I got all mixed up because I didn't know where I was in the air. When I was spinning, I kept my eyes open, which I usually don't do. It felt really weird and I was freaking out, thinking, How am I going to do this? So we studied the problem and realized that, when the television lights were set up and more people were in the stands to add color to the silver bleachers, the arena should feel more natural to me. I only hoped our theory was right. With the rib injury to contend with, we certainly didn't need any more problems.

Lloyd

As the first of our competitions drew nearer, we sat down and asked ourselves one last time if we were ready, and the answer was a definite yes. We had done everything possible to prepare, including identifying which moves would exacerbate Isabelle's injured rib. We also felt extremely confident about both our programs, especially the long, and knew they were a winning combination of artistic and technical moves.

For me, probably the most memorable experience of any Olympics is walking into the opening ceremony. The day before the competition was to begin, I stood outside the Olympic stadium with the rest of the Canadian team, and as we waited to march in with the other athletes, I thought about how meaningful this part of the Games was.

In my opinion, simply participating in the Olympics is far more important than winning the competition. The Games happen so rarely and the odds are definitely against you on one particular day that occurs once every four years. In other words, you can't count on winning. But you *can* count on the opening ceremony and the overwhelming pride you feel as you march in under your flag.

At the scheduled time of 4:00, the ceremonies began inside the stadium, which sat at the base of a mammoth ski jump. We excitedly awaited our entrance as Greece, in time-honored tradition, led off the parade of athletes. Our outfits were designed after the look of the RCMP and their colors of red, black and gold stood out brilliantly against the background of snow. Kurt carried the flag and we followed him in. That was the most exhilarating moment in the world to me as I felt the emotion well up inside. It must be the same for many of the other athletes because I saw a lot of people crying as they walked into the stadium.

Knowing that I was one of the few athletes who had been selected for the Olympics made it a proud day for me. Where it went from there was out of my hands. We could only try to do our very best and hope that everything went well. But I realized that winning a medal of any color couldn't compare to my experience at that moment. I was proud to be an Olympian and, more importantly, proud to be a Canadian.

After we had taken our seats, the president of the IOC came to the microphone and implored that the fighting in Sarajevo cease. Juan Antonio Samaranch then called for a moment of silence in remembrance of the war-torn city that had hosted the 1984 Olympics, and my own memories of the wonderful time I had there came rushing back.

I had walked into that Olympic stadium with all of the other athletes—the stadium that now served as a cemetery. I had skated at the Zetra where Scotty Hamilton and Katarina Witt had won their gold medals. It was a beautiful building and now, ten years later, it was a morgue. It was unbelievable that in such a short time a beautiful city like that could fall into utter shambles. During that moment of silence I mourned its loss.

Isabelle

When I walked into the stadium at the opening ceremony and saw all the people, I was overwhelmed. The spectators had been given white hooded ponchos to put on over their clothes and so the whole stadium blended in with the snowy landscape. I learned later that there were over 35,000 people in the stands.

Once the Games had been officially declared opened, I held my breath as the ski jumper flew through the air with torch in hand and made a perfect landing. The flame was then passed to a young, blind cross-country skier, who turned it over to the Crown Prince of Norway for the final lighting of the Olympic cauldron.

I looked at Lloyd, saw the thoughtfulness on his face and was so glad our relationship had arrived at such a peaceful place.

Lloyd

A typical day at the Olympics is pretty routine. Prior to competition, there is not much time for socializing. We were there to do a job, to get the work done, and our stringent schedule set the pace.

I was usually up by 7:00 a.m. and after breakfast would be on the bus to the arena by 8:15. Once at the rink, we would warm up and then practice from about 9:30 to 10:30. Then it was back on the bus and home to the village just in time for lunch.

After the meal I would usually relax by reading, playing a game of pin-ball or E-mailing, and then writing some postcards. Before long, I would be on the bus again for the second hour-long practice. If we rehearsed the short program in the morning we would rehearse the long in the afternoon. Back at the dorm, we would have dinner between 6:30 and 8:00 and be in bed by 11:30 p.m. The days leading up to a competition are not nearly as exciting as most people think, but this lifestyle is absolutely necessary to maintain the right frame of mind. Besides, there would be lots of time after we finished to socialize and take in the rest of the Olympics.

Isabelle

Our days at the Olympics leading up to the competition were very predictable. As a matter of fact, we lead a pretty quiet life months before the Games because we put in so much training during the day and are too tired by nighttime to even think of going out. It is like that for us from the moment we start to train in October until we finish competing in March.

The village in Hamar didn't offer much in the way of entertainment anyway, and because our competition was scheduled to be held early in the Games, we knew we would have two weeks after it was over to go out and have a good time.

Lloyd

Following my usual routine, on the day of the short program competition I didn't speak to anyone, not even my parents. They came to the first practice in the morning and, as always, wished me luck. I wouldn't see them again until that evening.

I slept for four or five hours before going on because I find sleeping is the easiest way for me to forget what was about to happen. When I awoke, I had a shower and went to the rink. Typically, I won't put my skates on until just before warm-up and I never come out of the dressing room until right before my name is announced. This drives my coaches crazy as they pace outside and repeatedly wonder aloud if I am ready.

I have never seen the point of working myself up into a frenzy before a competition. Nor do I sit down and visualize the program beforehand. I rely more on memory. In our sport, we often say there are "thinkers" and there are "natural" people, and I guess I'm one of the natural people. I just go out and do it. Sometimes I miss something and then I may ask myself why that happened, but I believe I'm a very consistent skater. When I'm on the ice, I know I'm prepared and so I just go out there and do it, time and time again.

Isabelle

Although I had tried hard not to think about it, I was still nervous as we began our short program. After all, this was to be the last time ever we would compete at the Games and, more than anything, I just wanted us to do the best we could. If we accomplished that, I really didn't care where we finished.

Earlier that day, I had been out to lunch with my family when my sister-in-law, Josée, looked at me in concern and asked if I was okay. In a sudden outburst, I had replied, "I must be crazy to be doing this to myself one more time! If I ever say anything about returning to the Olympics, just shoot me. I never want to be under this kind of strain again."

Just before I stepped onto the ice, I slapped my hands together in my usual fashion. "Come on, Iz," I said out loud, "you can do it," trying to give myself that extra boost of encouragement. From that moment on, I tried to forget about my sore ribs and the pressure of being at yet another Olympics. I had a job to do and I just wanted to get on with it.

Lloyd

As soon as we completed the double twist at the beginning of the program, the crowd began to clap. We went into our double Axels and, before I could see it, I realized Isabelle had landed the jump from the sound of the applause. Commentators, spectators, judges, coaches . . . everyone was watching Isabelle.

The first thing I said to her as we got back into hand-and-hand was, "Let's just concentrate." From there the program kept building and building, as each element was performed to the best of our ability. We finished, absolutely elated that we had done so well and skated to center ice to take our bows.

Coming off, I glanced at my partner and said, matter-of-factly, "You know we will be third." Long before the competition, we had guessed that our position was predetermined. But it really didn't matter. We had skated as we had wanted and were thrilled with the outcome.

After we received our marks, Rod Black, one of the television commentators and a good friend of the skaters, approached us with a microphone and said, "You know, you guys are probably going to be third."

Without thinking that we were on the air, I casually commented, "I don't really give a shit where we end up."

Isabelle looked at me and we both laughed. Then I turned back to Rod, and as I saw his chin drop and his mouth open, I suddenly realized that we must be live. He confirmed it when he said, "Well, we will go back upstairs to you . . ."

I received a lot of mail about that one. Isabelle is usually quite cautious about speaking out in public and is always telling me what I should or shouldn't say. But this time she wasn't upset at all because that is exactly how we both felt. The last two years had come down to that performance. We had done it and were satisfied. Where we finished in the rankings had no bearing on the high we were both experiencing. That I happened to accidentally share my feelings with viewers worldwide is another story and one that took me several months to live down.

Isabelle

I was so relieved after the short program was finished. My rib hadn't bothered me too much during our performance and we were just happy and proud of the way we had skated.

The next day at practice, we had to decide whether or not we were going to take out the triple lateral and whether my ribs should be taped during the competition. I said no on both counts. I knew that, although I was going to be in pain, I could make it through the program. I didn't want any elements left out and I thought the tape might affect my performance, as I had a difficult time breathing when it was on. Being in third after the short didn't automatically get us a medal. We could drop down in the standings quite easily, and although I didn't care where we ended up on the podium, I still wanted to be standing there when all was said and done.

We had a good practice the day of the long program, although we didn't do any more than necessary. I was experiencing some pain and the last thing we wanted was to aggravate my injury.

Lloyd

As we skated in the warm-up with the top Russian teams, I experienced a strange feeling seeing Gordeeva and Grinkov and Dmitriev and Mishkutenok. It had only been the year before when we had been on the Tom Collins tour together. Then we were friends and fellow workers having fun and enjoying the experience of the road. Now we were on the ice, competing against each other.

During the warm-up, we went through our usual ritual as we skated side by side, then parted to do our own thing. Isabelle ran through various elements while I just cruised around the ice to get my knees into it. I know if I am bending in my knees that I'm going to be fine. I have always relied on past experience and recognize the feeling I have to get in order to prepare myself to compete. Once this was done, we came together, performed a few elements and, although we may have had a couple of minutes left in the warm-up, we skated over to talk to Josée.

Taking advantage of the time, we wet our mouths using the toothpaste that we always have sitting on the boards. Nerves and a high altitude cause a dryness in the mouth that makes it difficult to breathe. We have found that a dab of toothpaste rubbed on the teeth creates saliva and combats the dryness. It was totally routine for us so you can imagine our surprise when, a few days before the competition, our toothpaste tube became a source of controversy.

It seemed that various officials thought, by displaying the tube on the boards, we might come across as endorsing the product, which is absolutely forbidden at the Olympics. They didn't want us to use the toothpaste at all while we were on camera. After much discussion, the conflict was finally settled when they allowed us to wrap duct tape around the tube, thus keeping the brand name hidden. Funny, but true.

When we stepped onto the ice to compete, the marks were coming up for the previous pair. I don't remember who they were because, frankly, I wasn't paying any attention. I skated around and looked for my parents, while Isabelle stood and spoke with Josée. As we approached each other, I noticed Isabelle talking to herself, as she always does. Just before we met, I looked up and asked for help. We came together, held hands and completed one little circle, during which time we offered each other words of motivation. Then we skated to center ice and, as we took our positions, Isabelle winked at me. It was her way of saying, "I am ready. Let's go have fun."

Isabelle

The first element we did in the program was our double Axel, followed by the triple lateral. The jumps were no problem but when I came down from the triple lateral, I hit my rib hard on Lloyd's shoulder. It hurt a lot and I wondered how I could complete the upcoming throw triple Salchow. I took a deep breath and somehow landed the throw.

Maybe it was the excitement of finishing those three difficult elements but, quite honestly, from that time until the end of the program I didn't feel a thing. I must have been blocking it out, though, because as soon as we stopped the pain returned in full force and I was sore for days after.

Lloyd

We had completed the performance of our lives and as I was on my knee, I put my hands together in relief and then looked up in gratitude. We had done it and had accomplished what we'd set out to do in the beginning—something that many thought we couldn't do and that we ourselves seriously doubted only twenty-four months before. With perseverance and much soul searching, we had found a way.

Isabelle pointed out a black Stetson that lay on the ice, which I immediately recognized. In a show of exhilaration, my dad had thrown his beloved hat to me and I skated over to pick it up and put it on. I couldn't see my parents from where we were standing, but when I watched the tape of our performance afterward, I realized how emotional it must have been for both of them. My mom couldn't even clap and seemed to be crying softly, while my father was on his feet for probably the last twenty seconds of the program. When I saw their reactions, it really touched me because their endless sacrifices and support had been crucial to my success.

As I watched the other winners skate out to the podium to collect their medals, I noticed that they didn't appear to be all that enthralled. Gordeeva and Grinkov had already won gold at a previous

Olympics, so it wasn't their first time, and Mishkutenok and Dmitriev were visibly upset because they thought they should have come in first. Suddenly a plan formulated in my head and I turned to Isabelle and said, "When we go out there, I am going to throw you on my shoulder and then spin around."

"What?" she responded, with a questioning look in her eyes.

"Just do it. Jump up there. We're not going to get another chance out here so let's enjoy it." I had let the moment slip by two years before by not appreciating my medal and I didn't want to make that mistake again. Besides, being the only pair in Canadian history to win two Olympic medals was something that I thought deserved at least a small celebration.

Isabelle laughingly agreed to my suggestion and as our names were called we went out and performed a spin that I don't think either of us will soon forget.

Isabelle

Once we knew that we had taken third place for certain, I said to Lloyd, Josée and Eric, "Well, finally we know how it *really* feels to win a bronze medal at the Olympics." Although we had ended up in the same position as we had in Albertville, this was a totally different experience and I don't think we could have been happier had we won gold.

My family were so excited for me. They knew how hard we had worked and all they had ever wanted was for me to be happy. I think that finally seeing a smile on my face made their joy complete.

The rest of the Olympics passed by fairly quietly for me. The morning after our competition, Lloyd and I refused to do any interviews and went to watch Jean-Luc compete. He hadn't done well in 1992, and as I watched him come down the hill, all I was hoping was that he would ski well and be as happy as we were. He deservedly won the gold and we were able to relax and enjoy the rest of the Games. Little did I know then that his win would contribute to our break-up in the near future.

One aspect of this Olympics that I thought was sad was the focus on the Nancy Kerrigan–Tonya Harding story. Nancy and I are good friends and normally we would have seen a lot of each other at a competition like this. But she wasn't allowed to go anywhere without a bodyguard. I could see how upset she was and received messages explaining that she wasn't allowed to come over and talk to us at various events. I felt so sorry for her.

Lloyd

I thought the media attention paid to the Kerrigan–Harding issue was a joke and I sympathized with Nancy because I didn't think she should have been put in that position. With respect to the people who did this to her, in my opinion anyone who stoops to those measures for personal gain, whether in sport, business or life in general, really has a problem. I believe, though, that what goes around, comes around, and you get what you deserve in the end. It was just unfortunate that Nancy had to suffer in the process.

I attended as many events at the Olympics as I could, in a very peaceful and content frame of mind. As I watched the Canadian hockey team take a silver medal and saw their heartbreak at losing the gold, I hoped that, in a few days time, they would appreciate their accomplishment. I knew what it was like to come third in 1992 and experience the incredible pain and disappointment of believing I had let so many people down. I also knew the feeling of being given another opportunity and then enjoying that same color of medal. I wanted to tell the hockey players that any medal won at the Olympics is gold. It just happens to be a different shade and it is attitude that determines the preciousness of the medal.

We were there to see speedskater Dan Janson win the men's 5,000 m race and witness the emotion in his triumph. To know what adversity Dan had gone through and then see his victory was heartwarming. If anyone deserved to win a medal, Dan did.

Seeing Elvis claim silver was fantastic and sharing in Kurt's huge disappointment after a disastrous skate in his short program brought us all a little closer together. I recall being in the team room with Isabelle and some of the others that night when Kurt walked in, looking quite somber. We sat and talked to him for hours, assuring him that his performance that day didn't define him as a person or as a skater. We emphasized that his achievements up to that point far outweighed the two and a half minutes he had spent out on the ice. Most of the team were in the room at various times and we all tried to support Kurt as much as possible. Two days later, it was a pleasure to watch him go out and perform his long program in a manner that befitted a four-time world champion. He skated great and we were all proud of our fellow Canadian.

Isabelle

By the time of the closing ceremonies, I was feeling a little sad because I knew that this Olympics was to be the last one, yet I was also happy it was over. Although we had tried to control the pressure at this Olympics, there was still a lot of stress attached to the Games and I'd had enough. I had done my job and finally skated the way I wanted to. In my mind, I knew I could never do another one.

With the Olympics finished, I flew with Lloyd to Toronto, where a press conference was being held for the returning athletes. Lloyd stayed on in that city for a couple of days while I returned home with the rest of the Quebec team. When we arrived, I couldn't believe the number of people at the airport to greet us. There must have been hundreds of well-wishers: the reception was amazing.

When Lloyd got back, we began training for Worlds almost immediately, as we wanted to be in top form for the last of our amateur competitions. It was important for us to end our careers on the highest note possible and our placement would also determine how many Canadian pairs teams would be sent to Worlds the following year.

Training was intensive yet we held back on the triple lateral. We didn't want to make my injury any worse than it already was and, in fact, we didn't actually try the throw again until practice at Worlds.

We arrived in Chiba, Japan, and a few days before competition I thought we should attempt the triple lateral. It had been two or three weeks since we had last performed one and I believed it was time. Lloyd was reluctant as he didn't think I was ready. But I insisted and the next thing I remember is coming out of the element in absolute agony. My rib had been hit again. The pain was much worse than it had been in the past and I began to cry. I couldn't breathe and every movement caused me to wince. I agreed for X rays right away, knowing that this time the injury was serious.

Lloyd

Isabelle's rib was cracked longitudinally. What had probably been a small fracture prior to the practice was now two inches in length and, due to the nature of the injury, would require complete rest in order to heal properly.

Practice was out of the question because it was just too painful for Isabelle. Once I realized her condition, I assumed that we would be withdrawing from the competition. In my mind it was a shame, though. We were the only world champions competing. Many of the other top skaters, including all the professionals who had been at the Olympics, had not shown up in Japan. But we had a legitimate reason to pull out and, under the circumstances, it seemed to be the only possible course of action. Everyone agreed—everyone, that is, except Isabelle, who informed us at a meeting that she was not about to quit.

Now, we hadn't skated the long program in its entirety for at least ten days. We had been missing practices and whole days of skating. Isabelle was in constant pain, not being able to breathe properly or sleep. This was not the perfect scenario. Yet my partner wanted to do this and, even though I thought she was crazy, I had to admire her courage. If it had been me with such an injury, I probably would not have gone through with the competition. I shouldn't have been surprised, though. Isabelle hadn't given up on anything we had done before. Why should she start now?

CHAPTER TEN

Going the Distance

Lloyd

ONCE I REALIZED her determination, I was ready to help Isabelle through it in any way I could. We took the day before the competition off and decided to take it all a step at a time. We would attempt the warm-up and, if it went well, we would compete in the short program.

On the day of our competition, we had a practice in the morning that was about average. The rib was definitely affecting how Isabelle could jump. She was falling on double Axels that she hadn't missed in eight months and I knew that was weighing heavily on her.

Isabelle

I think we were both a little nervous before the short program but our attitude was good. We were willing to accept the outcome, whatever happened. While we were taking our positions, Lloyd said to me, "If you get halfway through and have to quit, just stop. We will have given it our best shot."

"No," I replied. "We will keep going. We will do it."

Many people couldn't understand why I wanted to compete. They pointed out that we might not skate well, due to the injury, and drop below third. But I wasn't about to quit without even trying. I wanted to finish our amateur career the way it was intended. If we did poorly, I would know why. If I didn't attempt this, then I would never know what the outcome might have been. Lloyd said he would support me in any way he could and that was all I needed to hear.

Although I touched my hand down on the double Axel, we completed the rest of the program without any problem, and when we received our marks, we were sitting second behind the Russian pair, Shishkova and Naumov. I had been in considerable discomfort during the performance as I couldn't breathe properly when Lloyd caught me on the twist and also during the lifts. I was only able to withstand the pressure on my rib for so long. Yet, when we finished, we were elated with the results.

Once back at our hotel, I told everyone that I was going to bed because we had a practice in the morning. They all looked at me and said, "What?"

I replied, "I'm going to practice tomorrow." When they asked me why, I answered, "Because I'm going to be skating in the long tomorrow night." I guess everyone but me had assumed that we were finished.

The next day at practice, my coaches and Lloyd continued to try to convince me not to skate. I said, "You guys just don't understand. We *are* competing tonight."

Lloyd

At practice, I tried to talk Isabelle out of skating. I said, "We've proven we can do it. Let's just pull out now." But still she refused, and for most of the session was in tears from the pain and frustration of falling. Our routine had many tough elements and I really didn't know how she was going to be able to do it.

Isabelle had at least agreed to take out the triple lateral and do a double instead. Everything else was to remain in, and so it was with some trepidation that I began our program.

Our first element was the double Axel and Isabelle touched her hand down. I thought it was fantastic that she didn't fall and we continued on to the double lateral. As she landed, I could see the grimace on her face and could almost feel her pain. We then had to come around for a throw triple Salchow—the pinnacle of the program—and which Isabelle completed perfectly.

I asked her if she wanted to quit. She said, "No, keep going. Keep going."

From that point until the end of the program, I asked her the same question over and over again and each time she replied in the same way. Oddly enough, my worrying about Isabelle helped to take my mind off the fact that I was beginning to feel fatigued. Until we had actually stepped on the ice for warm-up, I had really believed that we wouldn't be skating so I hadn't prepared myself as well as I should have.

In the middle of the program, we were going into the throw triple toe, another element where I have to throw Isabelle by the rib. I suggested she do a double, to which she answered, "No way!"

Now I was really tired and as we were coming into the "Brasseur-Eisler" star lift, I thought we should only perform a normal star. In just three crosscuts, I tried to find out how Isabelle was and at the same time give her instructions on the next element. The only problem was, I had no air left in my lungs to speak properly and I wasn't sure if Isabelle understood me, so it was with some relief when I heard her reply, "Okay."

Somehow we continued, and with each jump and landing, the agony was reflected on Isabelle's face. Where she found the fortitude to perform these elements I will never know.

When we hit our final pose, Isabelle just buckled over. She was gasping for breath and sobbing. I had to hold her up and we could barely make it to center ice. We took a very forced bow and then I let her bow once by herself while I just stood and applauded Isabelle. I was in complete admiration—few people would have been able to do what she did. She just never gave up. Although many thought we should have come first that night, since the Russians didn't skate too well, the panel wasn't in our favor and we took silver. But we were happy. We knew we were one of the best teams and, if healthy, we could have won.

Isabelle

All the way through the long program, I just tried to block out the pain. Obviously, it never really went away, but somehow I was able to ignore it mentally. The second the music stopped, though, all of my strength left me. I couldn't even stand after the final position without Lloyd's assistance.

To make matters worse, I was selected for a drug test, which usually happens when an athlete is injured because they think you may have taken something for the pain. The strongest medication I had been given was Tylenol without codeine, which is perfectly acceptable to the ISU but did nothing to alleviate the pain of a cracked rib. As soon as I stepped out of the bathroom, my doctor was waiting for me with about ten pills to swallow.

I could barely stand on the podium but it felt good to have finished. It feels good now to know that I didn't quit. My partner had helped me through as I knew he would and we ended our amateur career in the best possible way. We hadn't given up.

Back at the hotel, we had a press conference to attend but my ribs hurt so much that I had to lie down on the floor during the questions and answers. My shoulders were uneven and, when I stood, I was leaning on one side, unable to walk straight. The painkillers didn't seem to be working and all I wanted to do was go to bed.

Lloyd

I felt so sorry for Isabelle. She couldn't even sit on a chair at the press conference and had to lie down. She was hardly able to speak.

One of the reporters asked the Russians if they had known about

Isabelle's injury and they answered no. I looked at them and thought, How could you not know? We had this problem for ten days. We were missing practices. Everyone at the World Championships knew. I was going to make a comment but changed my mind. Why waste my energy?

Someone else asked me, yet again, about the professional skaters being reinstated at the Olympics. Although I wasn't there to make a point, I did ask, "Did any of the professionals who returned to the Olympics show up at the World Championship?" I went on to say, "Everyone thought the pros were returning to do well and help their country out, yet in all cases 'substitute' athletes for the pros had to be sent to the Worlds . . . probably the same people who were supposed to have been at the Olympics." My statement seemed to quiet the reporters on that issue.

As far as Isabelle and I were concerned, this World Championship had been one more hurdle. We had accomplished what we had set out to achieve, battling a whole bunch of odds. Once again, we had survived.

Isabelle

I couldn't sleep that night. Every movement caused further pain and brought more tears to my eyes. It was about 3:00 in the morning when I finally gathered up my pillow and wandered down the hall to knock on Lloyd's door. When he answered, I said, "I skated for us last night and now you have to go through this with me."

He immediately made me comfortable on the couch and then sat beside me to rub my rib. When he saw the condition of the muscles in my back—one had apparently swelled an inch higher than the other—Lloyd called in the physio for a proper massage. My muscles were so swollen and tight. After that I was given more drugs and then Lloyd and I talked for at least an hour and a half before I went back to my room and passed out.

We didn't go on the ISU tour that year in order to give my injury time to heal. Instead we went straight home for a well-deserved rest and hoped that I would be sufficiently recovered for the Tom Collins tour, which we were scheduled to do the following month. Neither of us had discussed anything beyond that.

I was so happy everything was over and that finally I would be able to do things that I had always dreamt of. I figured I would go on tour and then have two whole months off. I was looking forward to enjoying a summer for the first time in my life, and although I knew I wanted to continue skating, the last thing I was thinking of was returning to the ice in September.

I was calm and sure about our impending retirement. I was ready, having done everything I had wanted to do. Sometimes, during all those years of competition, I would wonder what it was all for. Pairs skating is a hard sport on the body. Because I am not as strong as Lloyd, I always had to put myself at maximum strength and, for me, that was tiring. When I stopped, it was as if every part of my body thanked me. Finally, I didn't have to train for five hours a day and then go the gym and push myself to the edge. I was glad my amateur career was over. It was a tremendous relief to finish at last.

Lloyd

While at Worlds, we still hadn't decided what we were going to do in the future. We didn't know if there would be work for us or even if anyone would want us on the professional circuit. By the time of the tour, though, we had made up our minds that we would like to skate professionally but weren't sure what direction we should be taking. It was all so new to us. Our agent stepped in with various offers to skate in the fall and because we didn't know what to do or what not to do, we accepted everything.

Our official retirement was announced in July at a press conference in Toronto. At the same time, the CFSA unveiled the Brasseur-Eisler Award. The criteria stated: "This award may be given annually by the trustees to a pairs team in the Canadian Figure Skating Championships, novice, junior or senior, who during the course of the event demonstrated any one or more of the following in their performance . . . dedication to one another, overcoming adversity or obstacles, achieving a personal best, display of love and dedication for the sport." That was a proud moment for both Isabelle and me.

When the time came for us to speak to the press, I had no idea how difficult it would be to announce that we were turning professional. I stood and looked at the many reporters I had come to know over the years and suddenly got all choked up. I had to stop for a few seconds and fight back the tears before I was able to continue.

We were saying goodbye to a world that we had known for most of our lives . . . saying goodbye to all of our amateur friends, fans and competitions. It was a world that I had come to love and there was no question that I was going to miss it with all my heart.

EPILOGUE

Lloyd & Isabelle

THE SKATING WORLD lost a good friend in November 1995. Sergei Grinkov was one half of a great pairs team that, along with his partner and wife, Ekaterina Gordeeva, will be remembered for their grace, line and connection on the ice.

We loved competing against "G and G," as they were affectionately known, because they always brought our level of performance up a notch. Sergei's death has left a huge void in professional pairs skating. There is no one team that can do what they did or as well as they did it.

Adjusting to the professional world was hell. It took months before we adapted, and in the beginning we came very close to just bowing out. Slowly but surely, though, our new career gained momentum and we now think of ourselves as true professionals.

Touring in three separate shows a year, covering 105 cities across North America, isn't always easy. Include television specials, exhibitions, professional competitions and our own annual production of "Dreams on Ice" and suddenly you are leading a very hectic lifestyle.

Busy? Yes. Different from our amateur years? Absolutely. Routine? Not on your life! In fact, the stories we have gathered while skating in this "showbiz" setting could fill another book and, God willing, that is the plan.

But, in the meantime, we are loving every moment of what we do. The rules we once had to live by have been thrown out the window and we are finally free to skate the way we please. Ever trying to expand, we have invented more lifts unique to the Brasseur-Eisler team and are constantly striving to discover innovative ways to entertain. The only judge that is important now is the audience. When we receive approval from them, we are satisfied.

During our competitive years, we learned a great many lessons that we try to apply to our lives today. The medals that we won and continue to win are wonderful, but they are only objects. They sit somewhere in a box or on a shelf, gathering dust. It is the experiences, past and present, that we cherish. It is the people who have cared enough to influence who we are and what we do who are important. In our eyes, that is what life is about and what we truly hold dear.

Standing behind a black curtain at a skating rink, we wait for our names to be announced. As usual, we are closing the first half of the show. The crowd has already been entertained by some of the biggest stars in skating history and we are eager to get on the ice.

We hear the introduction and reach for each other's hand, gaining a certain comfort and security when we touch. Skating to center ice, a familiar excitement takes hold. For one brief moment, just before the music starts, there is silence, a transformation from reality to the illusion we hope to create. We stand poised and ready. A wink, a smile . . . and the magic begins yet again.

APPENDIX

Brasseur & Eisler's Awards and Achievements

Isabelle/Pascal Courchesne (1978-1986)

| Junior Worlds: | | 1985 – 6th |
| | | 1986 – 6th |

International:	St. Gervais	1984 – 5th
	Oberstof	1984 – 5th
	Skate America	1985 – 5th

Canadians:	(Novice Pair)	1983 – 2nd
	(Junior Pair)	1984 – 5th
	(Junior Pair)	1985 – 1st
	(Senior Pair)	1986 – 5th

Lloyd/Lorri Baier (1973-1982)

| Worlds: | 1982 – 8th |

Junior Worlds:		1978 – 6th
		1979 – 3rd
		1981 – 2nd
International:	St. Ivel	1980 – 1st
Canadians:	(Novice Pair)	1977 – 1st
	(Junior Pair)	1978 – 2nd
	(Junior Pair)	1979 – 1st
	(Senior Pair)	1980 – 2nd
		1981 – 2nd
		1982 – 2nd

Lloyd/Kathy Matousek (1982-1985)

Olympics:		1984 – 8th
Worlds:		1983 – 10th
		1984 – 5th
		1985 – 3rd
International:	St. Gervais	1982 – 2nd
	Oberstof	1982 – 2nd
	Skate Canada	1983 – 3rd
		1984 – 2nd
Canadians:		1983 – 2nd
		1984 – 1st

Lloyd/Karen Westby (1985-1986)

Canadians:		1986 – 3rd

Lloyd/Isabelle

Olympics:		
		1988 – 9th
		1992 – 3rd
		1994 – 3rd

Worlds:		
		1988 – 7th
		1989 – 7th
		1990 – 2nd
		1991 – 2nd
		1992 – 3rd
		1993 – 1st
		1994 – 2nd

International:	Prague Skate	1987 – 3rd
	Skate Canada	1988 – 1st
		1990 – 1st
	Trophée Lalique	1989 – 2nd
	NHK	1990 – 2nd
		1992 – 4th
		1993 – 1st
	Nations Cup	1991 – 1st
	Skate Electric	1989 – 1st
	Pireutten	1993 – 2nd

Canadians:		
		1988 – 2nd
		1989 – 1st
		1990 – 3rd
		1991 – 1st
		1992 – 1st
		1993 – 1st
		1994 – 1st

Non Skating Achievements & Awards

Quebec Figure Skating Federation Laureats:
    Best Pair 1988-1990 through 1994

Best Quebec Pair Athletes All Sports: 1988-1991-1993

Mcleans Honour Roll – 1993

Meritorius Service Medal (Government) – 1995

National Spokespersons for the Children's Wish Foundation since
    1992

Ambassadors for the Big Brothers/Sisters of Canada since 1994

Elected to the Canadian Sports Hall of Fame 1996

Co-producers of Dreams on Ice 1991 – present

Co-producers of Winter Dreams on Ice 1995 – present

INDEX